Cape Breton Shipwreck Stories

Cape Breton
Shipwreck
S T O R I E S

Collected by Ronald Caplan

Breton Books
Wreck Cove, Cape Breton Island

Compilation copyright © 1999 Breton Books

Editor: Ronald Caplan
Production Assistance: Bonnie Thompson
    and James Fader, Artplus

Front Cover Photograph: Helicopter lowering a man to the wreck of the *Gulf Gull*, ashore at Fourchu, February 1972. Photo by Ray Fahey for Abbass Studios. This photo won the Canadian Press Photo of the Month Award.

Back Cover Photographs: The *S.C. 709* encased in ice at Louisbourg, courtesy Jean Kyte. Survivors of the wreck of the *Kismet II*, Abbass Studio collection, Beaton Institute, University College of Cape Breton. The *Watford* ashore at Schooner Pond, courtesy Sara MacLean. The hand-coloured engraving is of the 1873 wreck of the *Adalia* on St. Paul's Island; the steamship *S.S. Pictou* rescuing the passengers and crew. The engraving was made from a sketch by an officer of the *S.S. Pictou*. The original is in the collection of Paul Cranford.

Photo Section: The graves of the victims of the *Dorcas-Etta Stewart* disaster are by Michael MacDonald. *Kismet II* and *Iceland II* photos, Abbass Studio collection, Beaton Institute. Euphemia Malcolm MacEachern was photographed by Carol Kennedy. Photographs of Ralph Rafuse and son, Walter Boudreau, Charlie Bagnell and Ed Levy, and John Angus Fraser, are by Ronald Caplan. Our thanks to Laura Peverill, librarian, University College of Cape Breton—a researcher's best friend.

2ND Printing 2001

LE CONSEIL DES ARTS DU CANADA DEPUIS 1957 | THE CANADA COUNCIL FOR THE ARTS SINCE 1957

We acknowledge the support of
the Canada Council for the Arts for our publishing program.

We also acknowledge support from Cultural Affairs,
Nova Scotia Department of Tourism and Culture.

Canadian Cataloguing in Publication Data

Cape Breton shipwreck stories

  ISBN 1-895415-48-9

FC2343.7.S5C36 1999   971.6'9   C99-950236-0
G525.C36 1999

Contents

Introduction

by Ronald Caplan, Wreck Cove

SOMETIMES I THINK the best thing to come out of a shipwreck are the stories people tell. Gathering stories for this new collection, I realized that there are lots of ways to tell a shipwreck story, and lots of people ready to tell them—from those who were on board to those who tried to rescue them to those who boarded the abandoned wreck after the storm died down. And there are people like Elva Jackson and Sara MacLean and Mike MacDonald, people who, years later, determine to put a shipwreck back together, to read everything and talk to everyone and make of what they find one able story.

Cape Breton Shipwreck Stories is a collection of good stories told in a variety of ways, from eyewitness accounts to well-researched essays, from fiction to song—the voices of survivors, and across-the-kitchen-table memories of those who were on shore. Ralph Rafuse and John Angus Fraser take us on board the *Iceland II* at Fourchu and the *Kismet II* at Meat Cove. Walter Boudreau carries us from the rescue of American seamen trapped in an ice-clad vessel at the mouth of Louisbourg Harbour to, a short time later, his days adrift in a lifeboat after a Nazi submarine sank the barquentine *Angelus* in the mid-Atlantic. And Euphemia MacEachern, Lillian Crewe Walsh, and K.D. MacAskill keep the memory of tiny, tragic events alive in poetry and song.

I am struck by the devotion to detail some people bring to reconstructing such events. Mike MacDonald pieced together the wrecks of the *Dorcas* and the *Etta Stewart* out of Louisbourg memories and the newspapers of the day, visiting graveyards and following the movement of the bodies, putting it all together for us much as did the Inquiry of the day, sailing over the spot in a glass-bottomed boat and inspecting the rope to determine was it torn or deliberately cut—and what that said about the wreck, and what that information means. It is a wonderful piece of detective work—theirs, one hundred years ago, and Mike's.

It's no surprise that Cape Breton Island should have a wealth of good shipwreck stories. The marvel is that so many people troubled to share the tales, to remember, research and record. Reading these chapters I realize that they are only a taste of Cape Breton's shipwreck experiences, and I am once again grateful for those who keep such lamps lit, and for how these stories teach, humble, encourage and entertain us poor creatures on the shore.

Journal of the Voyage and Wreck of the *Auguste*, 1761

by Saint-Luc de la Corne

Here is a traditional shipwreck narrative in which a survivor recalls details of the wreck, "the various routes he took in getting back to his homeland, and of the privations and sufferings he endured in this distressing catastrophe." The *Auguste* was carrying French passengers heading back to France after the fall of Canada to the English. There were 123 aboard, including women and children. Saint-Luc de la Corne was a fifty-year-old merchant, soldier, and fur trader, and a member of the Chivalrous Order of Saint-Louis. The exact location of the wreck—on November 14, 1761, at Dingwall Harbour in northern Cape Breton—was not discovered until 1977. See **Notes**, page 127.

I LEFT MONTREAL on September 27, 1761, in the schooner *Catiche*, Captain Dussaut, accompanied by my brother the Chevalier, my two children, my two nephews, and several other French officers and soldiers. We got as far as Three Rivers on the 28th, left there on the 29th, and were lucky enough to reach Quebec on the same day.

General Murray received us with all possible politeness. He spared no pains to assure us of a pleasant crossing, and we were quite overcome by his efforts on our behalf. Only two vessels had been provided to take our party to Europe. Perceiving that these were not adequate—for they could not comfortably take such a large number of passengers—I suggested to General Murray that I should buy or hire another vessel at my own expense. He turned down the suggestion, out of generosity it seems, for two days later the ship *Auguste* was made ready for us. I engaged her stateroom at a cost of five hundred Spanish piastres, which I paid over to the captain.

On October 11, after discussing with my brother the danger to which we would be exposed because of the captain's not being a pilot, we called on General Murray to ask his permission to engage a river pilot. The General replied that we would be in no more danger than the other vessels, since he was sending a small boat with instructions to escort us all down as far as the last anchorage on the river.

A strong northeast wind held us in harbour for three days. We got away on the 15th, but went only to St. Patrick inlet. On the following day, with a southeast wind, we hoisted anchor and reached a point about a league from the Isle aux Coudres, where the strength of the current forced us to anchor. As we did so, the ship's big anchor gave way; the anchorage itself was not at all safe, and very little would have sufficed to throw us on shore. We were on the verge of being wrecked, and this would have been rather to our liking, for we were still within the borders of Canada.

We set off again on the 17th, and came to anchor with the two other vessels in the good harbour of Isle aux Coudres. We were not able to go further until October 27, being delayed by a strong northeast wind. In the intervening time we consumed the greater part of our provisions and had to buy fresh supplies at heavy cost. At length, favoured with a southwest wind, we got to a point opposite Camouraska, where we anchored.

The next day, October 28th, the wind holding firm, the officer appointed to escort us withdrew from all three vessels the guards he had posted there. Then with a fair wind we parted company. We kept on our way with the other two ships, though these were soon lost to view. We estimated on the night of November 1 that we had gone twenty-two leagues on the two previous days, October 30th and 31st. The *Jeanne* came up with us in the morning and told us she had spoken to a ship out of London, commanded by Captain Benjamin Nulton. She gave no particulars and we parted company again.

On the 2nd and 3rd of November we made way with a north

2

wind. Up till now we could not complain of sailing conditions. Everything seemed to promise a good crossing, the inclement season notwithstanding.We were enjoying perfect weather when, on the fourth day of the month, a most violent northeast wind blew up. The sails were reefed, the helm made fast. Every instant we seemed to see our graves yawning to receive us. The pitching of the ship was so violent that the ropes holding our trunks were broken, belaying pins were torn out, and several on board were disabled or wounded by tossing and tumbling trunks, boxes and valises.

The storm lasted from the fourth of the month to the sixth. The consternation of the passengers can be imagined, as well as the bitter exhaustion of the crew, exposed as they were for forty-eight hours, without let-up, to all the rigor of a frightful and unending storm. What vows ascended to Heaven! What promises!... And, I may add, What profanity! And the Supreme Being answered this once the prayers of the good people who called on Him..., and we were delivered by His All-Powerful Hand from the fate we thought inevitable.

Calm weather followed the gale, and all hands worked together to repair the damage that the ship had sustained. We forgot all about danger, we were all in fine fettle, each trying his best to outdo the other. But scarcely had we got straightened away when a new mishap put us in the utmost danger.

Twice before the ship had caught fire in the galley, but each time we had put out the blaze quite easily. On the 7th we were working our hardest and the cook, perhaps to give us more energy, was doing his best to cook more food or to cook it more quickly. For the third time fire broke out, and we were on the point of falling from Charybdis into Scylla. Had it not been for combined efforts of captain, passengers and crew, we would certainly have been consumed by fire in the middle of the ocean.

We succeeded with much difficulty in putting out the blaze, but the ship had been considerably damaged. Ordinarily the damage would not have mattered too much, but we had terrible things in store for us. The cries of the women on board, and the wailings of several men whom the prospect of imminent danger had unnerved, pierced the hearts of all of us, and we knew a fear that we were unable to dispel.

To make matters worse, lack of food had sapped our strength. For all this time we had been obliged to exist sparingly on biscuits, since we were unable to do any cooking. Such food did nothing more than to prevent us from dying. On top of all this, we were all bedridden with seasickness.

After a short spell of fine weather, a strong east wind blew up on the 9th and carried us to the Driser Islands, where we gave wide berth to Bird Island. The wind blew steadily until nine o'clock on the morning of the 11th, by which time we were in sight of Newfoundland.

Fine weather made it possible to take some soundings, and at our instigation the captain did so. We found ourselves in 43 fathoms on Orphans' Bank. Although we were spent with fatigue, the prospect of fresh supplies set us all to fishing—and the fishing was good. This period of calm almost made us forget the dangers through which we had passed, for with two hundred codfish on board we were certain at least of not dying of hunger. We had lost much of our food supplies in our different mishaps.

The spell of fine weather was soon over. An east wind with gales and drenching rain drove us before we knew it to the coast of Isle Royale [Cape Breton Island]. We were within an ace of destruction. The night was so dark we became aware of an enormous cliff just as we were about to be dashed against it. The crew, goaded to unusual effort by the instant peril, parried the blow as much by good luck as by skill, for we went past no more than a gunshot from the rocks. To avoid the shoals, we were obliged to tack to the northeast for five or six hours during the night.

About ten o'clock on the morning of the 12th we sighted land. What efforts we could make to keep offshore were weak and ineffective. About two o'clock we were near to being carried ashore, and the captain at our insistence dropped anchor. Fortunately it held. And then the same Divine Hand that had before delivered us from disaster favoured us with an auspicious wind. This saved us, for the coast was so near, and so exceedingly dangerous, that we must inevitably have come to grief. We beat off the wind and got away from a shore on which we would certainly have perished.

On the night of the 12th the wind swung to the east. We rounded the cape and stood a tack to the north for some hours. Then we came about and, on the night of the 13th, tacked to the southeast. These maneuvres we made with no inkling of where we were, since the weather was always lowering, with heavy rain.

Our distress can well be imagined. We were uncertain of our whereabouts and without food. The crew, fifteen including the captain, mate, coxswain and deck hands—two of whom were disabled—were in the depths of despair. Some of the soldiers were worn out from endless work and loss of sleep, six having been assigned by the captain to each watch. We ourselves were exhausted for the same reasons, for in maneuvering the ship everyone did as much as he could to help out; although we were not very expert at the business, the sailors were nonetheless buoyed up by our endeavours, and we were the less dejected.

On the night of the 14th we were still in sight of land but could not recognize it, having on board only maps of Europe. We kept well off, drifting at the mercy of wind and storm. The storm increased in fury. The crew, drained of strength, lost all heart and took the unhappy course of climbing into their hammocks to get some rest. This desperate action cost them their lives.

We could no longer see any hope of saving ourselves. The captain and mate used every conceivable argument to persuade the men to make one last effort. All urging was in vain. The mate, an energetic fellow, tried to rouse them from their hammocks by using a stick, but his efforts were futile. The crew in very truth were already dead men. Exhaustion and the spectre of certain disaster had taken the life out of them.

Resolute and firm, the mate went up to the bridge. I was already there with the captain and two others, the man at the helm and one of my servants. "It is impossible to work the ship," said the mate. "Our mizzenmast is broken, our sails are in shreds and can be neither brailed up or lowered away. The crew have yielded to despair and are sunk in torpid slumber, certain of death; they have chosen their lot. As for us, we can't of our own efforts keep the ship heading into the wind. As a last resort we've got to make for shore."

We could see land on both sides of us, and thought we could make out a river about half a cannon shot away. The time had come for desperate measures. The captain and mate, gazing at me with distrait eyes, joined their hands in prayer. I knew well enough that our plight was serious, but this gesture shook me to the marrow, and I stood there speechless. I threw off my lethargy when the mate shouted to the captain: "We have no other course—and not a minute to lose. It will be safer to hit the shore on the starboard side." It did look less dangerous in this quarter, for what seemed to be the mouth of a river offered some hope that we could save ourselves. Had it been navigable we might have made our way in safety. The captain agreed to make the attempt, since he could think of nothing better. He knew it was our only hope and that it had to be attempted. I awoke to our peril when the captain and mate, turning to me with lifeless eyes and praying hands, warned me to expect the worst. I decided then to tell the passengers of the desperate but inevitable decision that the captain and mate had taken. There was nothing else to be done; our fate was decreed, and only the hand of Providence could save us.

I told my brother of our sad lot. Then I went below and told the passengers of both sexes of the danger that threatened, of the decision of those in command, of the crew's utter despair.... Already the ship was drifting towards the shore.... What prayers went up to God! What promise and vows! Vows and promises, alas, that were all in vain! The fatal moment came on apace.

All our efforts went to reach the mouth of the navigable river, each of us expecting every moment to be his last. Who could describe the violence of the waves in the instant that we struck! Time after time the tips of the masts seemed to rake the very clouds, and time after time we thought ourselves swallowed in the abyss.

Once grounded, our first care was to cut away the masts and rigging from the down side of the ship. We got this done, but the violence of the waves threw her on her beam ends. We were roughly between 120 and 150 feet from land; and on a sandy bar that completely shut off the entrance to the little river! The ship was so damaged that she was half under, and passengers of both sexes had to clamber up to the bridge. Some, driven witless by the danger they were in, and thinking they could make it safely to shore, threw themselves into the water, and so perished. The rest took up positions near us, clinging to shrouds and back-stays, and tried to hold on against the waves that rolled over us, one hard upon the other. Several were swept away, and this was not to be wondered at in men so completely done in.

We still had the two ship's boats—our last resort. But this ray of hope, having sustained us amid the violence of the waves, was soon extinguished, for the larger of the two boats was swept away by the waves and smashed to fragments. At the same instant the smaller boat was thrown into the water.

A servant of Mr. Laveranderie by the name of Etienne instantly threw himself into the boat; the captain and some others followed. I saw what was going on when one of my children that I held in my arms, and young Henry, who was fastened to my belt, cried out: "Save us, save us! The boat is in the water." Without an instant's hesitation I grabbed a rope and slid down to a nearby opening: then, with a violent effort, I threw myself clear and fell by good fortune into the boat. In so doing I lost my son and little Henry, for they were not strong enough to follow me. Though we were in the lee of the ship, a wave filled the boat almost to the top; a second carried us away from the ship. I had the presence of mind to climb up on the edge of the boat and in an instant a third wave threw me up on the beach.

It would be difficult to do justice to the horror of my situation: the cries of those who remained on the vessel; the futile efforts of those who, hoping to save their lives, threw themselves into the sea; the cold and drenching rain; the certainty that I had lost my children. Those who, like myself, had been thrown ashore were in a fainting condition, prostrate from exhaustion on an unknown shore.

The captain, stretched out on the beach, was the first I tried to help. I managed to get some water out of him and give him some relief; but he was out of his head and seemed to have difficulty in getting back to normal. I did my best to help some of the others and had good success, but I had to work slowly and painfully for my own strength was almost gone. Alive on the shore were only seven of us: the captain; Laforet, corporal in the Roussilon regiment; Monier, a corporal from Bearn; Etienne, a servant; Pierre, a servant; Laforce, a discharged soldier; and myself.

Anxious not to lose sight of the vessel, I gave my powder horn, ramrod and flint—articles I had fortunately been able to save—to five of the men so that they could make a fire at the edge of the woods, distant three-quarters of an arpent from the shore. They had no success, they were so completely chilled and exhausted; they hardly had courage enough to come and tell me of their failure. I went along at once and succeeded after many attempts in making a fire. It was nearly time, for already the poor fellows could hardly move or talk. They would certainly have perished without assistance.

The heat soon brought them round. The captain, seemingly the most affected, came to himself and told me he was not at all sure of where we were, but that he thought us to be in the vicinity of Louisbourg. He gave himself entirely to my direction, and the confidence he seemed to have in me encouraged me to carry on.

We had been thrown ashore between two and three o'clock in the afternoon. Between five and six the ship went to pieces on the shore, and we beheld the distressing spectacle of lifeless bodies washed ashore, one hundred and fourteen in all. Following are the names of those who perished:

Captains: MM. Le Chevalier de la Corne, Becancourt Portneuf.

Lieutenants: MM. Varennes, Godefroy, Laveranderie, Saint-Paul, Saint-Blain, Marole, Pecaudi de Contrecoeur.

Foot Ensigns: Villebond de Sourdis, Groschaine Rainbaut, Laperiere, Ladurantaye, Despervanche the younger.

Cadets: MM. La Corne de Saint-Luc, Chevalier de la Corne, La Corne Dubreuil, Senneville, Saint-Paul the younger, Villebond the younger.

Bourgeois: Paul Hery, Francois Hery, Lechelle, Louis Hervieux. Mesdames de Saint-Paul, Mesiere, Busquet, Villebond; Mlles. de Sourdis, de Senneville, Meziers.

An English merchant named Delivier, the mate, three officers, the maitre-d'hotel, eight sailors, two deck hands, and the cook.

Twelve women, wives of merchants or of soldiers.

Seventeen children, eight artisans or farmers, thirty-two soldiers.

We spent a night of great sadness. Our dismay was so heavy that we scarcely spoke to one another. Our utter exhaustion must have put us to sleep, otherwise it would not have been possible to close an eye. On the morning of the 16th we went down to the beach, where we found the bodies of our unfortunate companions in disaster. Some were naked, having doubtless thrown off their clothes the better to save themselves in the waves. Of some the legs and other limbs had been broken. We spent the day in giving them what burial our desperate straits and our strength made possible.

We decided we must leave a place where we had always before our eyes the spectacle of death. On the 17th, having gathered provisions strewn along the shore, we loaded ourselves with rations for eight days only—all except the soldiers who, thinking themselves not too far from inhabited regions, took food for only three or four days. In spite of our warnings, they loaded themselves with useless articles that they had to throw away after three or four days. I did my best to convince them that I had had too much experience not to fear the fatigue and hardship I could see lay in store for us. Obsessed with greed, they were deaf to all advice.

We started off quite at random, for we knew neither where we were nor where we were going. We traveled four days—over sheer cliffs whose hideous aspect dismayed us; through forests whose denseness frightened us; over rivers whose swiftness hindered our march; over mountains so difficult to climb that we lost all heart.

On the 21st, as a crowning misfortune, snow covered the land. In spite of careful rationing, our supplies were near depletion, and we were weakened by a journey so arduous. Courage was at low ebb, and three of the party, weakened by too little food and on their last legs from weariness, resolved to stay where they were. They preferred certain death to sufferings to which they could see no end.

I was able by my exhortations, and by hopes that I held out to them that our ordeal would soon be ended, to get them going again. We came on the 25th to Niganiche [present-day Ingonish], where we found some small deserted houses in which lay the bodies of two dead men.

It seemed that bad luck would never weary of pursuing us. The man called Etienne fell sick of pleurisy. The only remedy I could

9

think of was to bleed him, and I repeated the treatment six times during the night, using the point of a knife. I also made him sweat three times. By these hazardous measures he was considerably relieved. He was too feeble, however, to continue the journey.... He had to be left behind. Monier offered to stay with him; he was by no means as sick as Etienne, but was at least as tired and discouraged.

We left them on the 26th, after assuring them that at the first inhabited region we reached I would arrange for all necessary help to be sent to them, and that I would spare nothing in rescuing them. I left them about four pounds of flour, two cooked fowls, about a pound and a half of lard, and half a pound of broken biscuits. They had no pot for cooking, but they did have a silver goblet.

During the night some ten or twelve inches of snow had fallen, but this did not deter us. The cabins gave us hope that we would soon find something better, but the snow hid from us any trails there might have been. We had much to endure, for there were many rivers which we had difficulty in crossing. No one else would lead the way, so I always went first. Often I had to return to take over the packs before I could get the others to follow. This was true of all except the captain who trusted entirely in me and did exactly as I instructed. The others declared a thousand times that they would rather perish than continue a journey so exhausting. They were so much demoralized that I had to make shoes for them and often to carry their packs.

We continued our journey through woods and mountains until the third of December, when we came to the Bay of St. Ann. There were only five of us, and we still had no knowledge of where we were. We found a shallop on the north bank of the channel, apparently long since abandoned. It was high and dry on the end of a sandbar. This discovery gave us new hope, but we were less sanguine when we saw that the boat lacked three planks and was almost rotten.

There was nothing for it but to work on the boat and get it in shape to make the crossing, about 1200 feet. The captain, expert in such matters, was of great help. We made camp on the end of the bar and worked to the limit of our strength in repairing the boat.

The work was hardly completed when a northeast wind accompanied by heavy snow put us in miserable straits. We all but perished from cold. We had only barrel staves for fuel and the heavy snowfall kept extinguishing our little fire.

In such miserable circumstances the dearth of provisions filled up the measure of our misfortunes. For food we had only one and one-half ounces per day of spoiled provisions, except that we sometimes found some red seeds called rose hips and some seaweed known as *baudy*. These quieted the pangs of hunger, but left us weakened.

On the 4th of December the storm died down and we found our shallop covered deep in snow. We made superhuman efforts to get it into the water, and finally succeeded. This did us little good, however, for the captain, who up till then had kept up a good front, declared that he could not possibly go further. Not only was he very weak, but the pain that he was suffering in his legs, all torn and festered, had given him a high fever. The three Frenchmen, almost as sick, applauded his decision. Finding myself alone, I had to agree to remain with them, although I was much less afflicted than the others. I did not want to abandon them, and so we rested in Providence.

A few minutes after we had made our fateful decision, two Indians came upon us. Their coming was announced by the joyful shouts of my companions, who ran to them with outstretched arms, tears preventing them from speaking. I could hear their sepulchral voices, choked with sobs, babbling these words: "Have pity on us! Have pity on us!"

I smoked away at my pipe, looking quietly on at this moving scene. My companions pointed me out and explained that I had led them thither, but that they no longer had strength to follow me. The two Indians came over to me, and shook hands. They did not recognize me for some time, so greatly was I changed by my long beard and my emaciated condition. On more than one occasion I had done a good turn for this people, so I was given a hearty welcome.

I asked how far we were from Louisbourg. The Indians told me that we were within thirty leagues of the place, and that they were ready to take me to St. Peters. I accepted their offer with a full heart. After transporting the captain and three Frenchmen to the other side of the channel, I made them a good fire and left them the little flour and fat that was left—enough to make them a scanty meal. Then I set out with the two Indians for their cabin, situated on the bay about three leagues from where we were.

I was very well received there. The Indians shared with me what little meat they had. It was only dried meat, but they gave me enough for two days. On the morning of the 5th I set out again with my two savages to return to my companions. We took with us two birch-bark canoes, and we all set off for St. Peters. We succeeded in getting round Cape St. Ann in a strong northeast wind, and entered the bay of La Brador. Here, because of wind and snow and rain, we were held up for two and a half days, during which time we ate up all the dried meat the Indians had given us.

We finally arrived, at midnight on the 8th of December, at St. Peters. Here we found five Acadian households, comprising in all ten persons. I immediately sent off the two Indians to go to the rescue of the two poor Frenchmen I had left at Niganiche. I gave them twenty gold louis, 80 pounds of flour, fifty pounds of lard, tobacco, powder, lead, a silver cup, and many other things I had. They promised me they would make all possible despatch in going to save the men. But in spite of all my efforts I doubted that they would find them alive.

We took two and a half days to get rested and lay in supplies. On the 11th I wrote a letter to the governor of Isle Royale, informing him, without going into much detail, of our shipwreck. I explained to him that I wanted to make the most of the closing season to cross from Isle Royale to Acadia; once there I would give every effort and employ every means to get back to my homeland. In earnest of what I said in my letter, I sent to him the captain of the ship and the two French soldiers, La Foret and Laforee, with two Acadians as guides. On parting with me the captain was deeply moved. He wanted me to go with them and did everything he could to persuade me to do so. He pointed out the difficulty of reaching Canada in such a hard season. But his arguments fell on deaf ears; my mind was made up. I had undergone too much suffering to expose myself to new tribulation. I shared with him the nine guineas I had left, and he seemed to appreciate my thoughtfulness. But I was just as glad to render service to him as he was to receive it.

My intention of crossing to the mainland frightened the Acadians, and I succeeded in persuading them to take me over only by offering them money. I acquired a small birch-bark canoe, the lure of 25 louis persuaded two young men, and we set off. There were four of us in the canoe counting Pierre, like myself a survivor of the shipwreck. On the 12th we slept at the home of a man called Abraham on the far side of St. Peter's portage.

On the night of the 13th of December the weather became calm, so we embarked for the crossing and arrived safely at Cheda-Bouctou. We stayed with a man called Joseph Maurice in a settlement of nine Acadian cabins. I betook myself as soon as I could to the head of the bay, where I engaged some Indians to make snowshoes for us. We set off again on the 15th and traveled three days to reach the home of Jacques Cote at Pommiquet, a settlement containing five Acadian households. Here I was obliged to leave Pierre, who could go no further on snowshoes.

We arrived on the 18th at Artigongne where we found five huts of Indians literally dying of hunger—and we had no supplies to spare. Here I engaged two guides to take me to Picton. The cold was so severe that we got there only after three days traveling, though the distance was not great. We found no better hosts here, for Indians here were also starving.

We set off again on the 21st and followed along the sea to Tectemigouche where we arrived much exhausted on the 24th. I stayed in this place to get my strength back. On the 5th of January, 1762, I sent off two couriers to the commandant at Fort Cumberland. I reported to him of the dire straits to which I was reduced by shipwreck and by the hard traveling I had done in such severe weather. I asked him to send me some food supplies to enable me to reach the fort.

We were on our last legs from exhaustion and lack of food. Our hungry stomachs easily digested the disgusting flesh of a skinny fox that we killed on the 6th; only its bones were left. We came to our senses on the 7th, when an English sergeant, commanding a detachment of 12 or 15 men at Bay Verte, heard of our situation and sent me a bottle of wine, some lard, and some cooked meal. This food gave us back some strength, and we got through to the post about noon.

We were received with much consideration. The sergeant very generously shared with us an abundance of good things that he had for himself. I was well aware that I owed my very life to his kind attentions. About two o'clock I set off for the fort, some five leagues away—far enough for an exhausted man. Happily, the commandant for Fort Cumberland had sent off a wagon loaded with provisions, escorted by a soldier and one of my messengers. Meeting them, I decided to spend the night in the woods. My weariness drove me to get some rest and the good things to eat impelled me to make up the sleep I had long gone without.

Next day I set out in the wagon and arrived at the fort. I was flattered at the welcome accorded to me. The commandant, his officers, the townspeople and merchants expressed their regret for the loss I had sustained in the shipwreck and their pleasure at my having survived. The commandant, whose name was Benoni Danks, placed a room at my disposal, and procured for me all available comforts that one could desire. I lacked for nothing necessary or useful that he was able to get for me.

On the 14th of January I left the fort, overwhelmed with best wishes and filled with thankfulness. I had supplies for 15 days, sufficient to carry me through to Father Germaine's at Haut Paques. We arrived there on the 29th, by way of the portages of Miramigouchir, Miniagouche and by the Peshoudiar. We followed this latter river for three days. We got through just in time, for snowshoes and provisions were about done—and our endurance as well. Father Germaine had in the way of food only some Indian corn. He gave me two bushels which, with a little lard that was left of what we had received from the commandant of Fort Cumberland, decided us to continue our journey. We left Father Germaine's on the 2nd of February and followed St. John River as far as the Great Falls. From there we went by way of the portage of Themiscouata, where I had to leave behind the two Acadians who had accompanied me on the trip. I made my way quickly to Kamouraska, from which place I sent out a wagon to bring in the Acadians. The long journey, altogether on snowshoes, with all its discomforts and privations, had completely exhausted them. We reached Quebec on the 23rd, but this part of our journey was much less fatiguing. Carriages and food were easily available.

I reported at once to His Excellency General Murray and gave him my account of the shipwreck. I set out for Montreal and arrived on the 24th, when I also reported to General Gage and sent Major Dezeney a copy of my journal.

It would be difficult to recount all the hardships I went through. The hard experience of the shipwreck itself was almost forgotten in the further difficulties I encountered in getting back to my homeland. I declare that the more I go over in my mind the circumstances of my shipwreck and of my safe delivery the more I am amazed.

I believe that, with all the detours I had to make, I must have covered at least 550 leagues—and this in the hardest of all seasons, and without help. I saw my guides and companions, whether Indians or Acadians, after eight days on the trail—or even less—physically incapable of going further. During the whole time I enjoyed perfect health. I was afraid that my constitution would be undermined, but I came through all my privations in good condition. If I had had guides as vigorous as myself I would not be so much out of pocket, for I spent 130 louis on guides; besides, I should have made the trip back to Quebec more quickly.

I have not intended to give a full account of the shipwreck and of the events that followed it. I have merely recounted the main circumstances, and this without embellishment. I do not set myself up to be an author, and Truth has no need of adornment.

Wreck of the *Astraea* at Little Lorraine, 1834

Here are two documents that take us into the world where the *Astraea* came ashore, on May 8, 1834. We have a survivor's letter home. But first, there is the report from H.W. Crawley to the Provincial Secretary of Nova Scotia, pleading for aid for the people of Little Lorraine. The residents of that community had gone to so much trouble to assure proper burials for the *Astraea* victims that they themselves now faced a bleak winter. Crawley's report "sets in bold relief not only the necessary details of the wreck itself but also the whole problem of dealing with shipwrecks at that date." See **Notes**, pages 132-133.

from H. W. Crawley's Report

I AM JUST RETURNED from the scene of a terrible shipwreck, that of the barque *Astraea*, W. Ridley master, with passengers from Limerick for Quebec. She struck on rocks under Little Loran head (between Manadou and Louisbourg) close to the shore, in a very dark night, and went to pieces immediately, only 3 persons escaping out of 251. These 3 were the surgeon, by name O'Sullivan, the carpenter, and one seaman. They leaped into the sea as the ship was parting, and were washed by the tremendous surge on to the top of the precipice. All the rest went to the bottom, in about 18 feet water tho', as before said, quite close to shore. The cabin passengers, beside the surgeon, were a Mr. O'Doherty, who it is reported was one of Lord Almer's suite, on his way to Quebec; an old maiden lady, whose name I have not learned, going to her brother, in Canada; and a young woman named Moss, from Limerick. The rest were steerage passengers, and, as I understand, consisted of farmers and their families, from the vicinity of Limerick.

Wreck of the Astraea, 1834

This is by far the most disastrous wreck that has occurred on our coast this season, and there have been 6 or 7 already. My reason for addressing you is to enquire what hopes there may be of obtaining remuneration for the people who are employed in the very necessary business of securing and interring the dead bodies. There are but few persons living in the immediate neighborhood, and they are poor fishermen who are now particularly hurried to get their potato seed into the ground, and to attend to their fishery, this being the principal season. The process at the wreck is so tedious that it seems probably the delay will be so great as to cause the loss of their usual harvest, both on land and sea. I found these poor fellows, to the number of about 15, part in boats dragging for the bodies, and part on shore excavating the ground, for which they had very poor instruments; a few Irish spades and no pickax. They had been at this work, I believe, about fifteen days, and had got up and interred about 70 or 80 bodies. They were growing very tired and disheartened, seeing the alternative was the loss of their crops and fishing without any certainty of being paid for the work they were performing, or of leaving the corpses to be strewed along the coast, a prey to the pigs, dogs, fish &c, &c. They found, too, that with their limited numbers and means it was hardly possible to finish before the bodies would be in so advanced a state of decomposition that to manage them would be exceedingly difficult, for they were already changing fast.

I should have been very glad that I could have assured them of remuneration, and set them to work heartily, with proper tools and more laborers. As it was, I stretched my conscience a little by telling them I thought it impossible they could be refused payment. You will think, perhaps, as I have heard some persons intimate, that the men would take care to pay themselves from the wreck, and the property of the deceased. That, I verily believe, is impracticable. The wreck was bought by one person, who, being always in attendance, keeps all that has escaped destruction for himself. This is not much. The hull, masts, crates, boxes, and everything that would float, were dashed to a thousand atoms among the rocks. All that would sink is at the bottom in 18 feet of water. Coins, of course, can never be recovered. Cordage and iron work the purchaser rakes up, and also some clothes, paltry enough. He does not pretend to claim what is found on the bodies; but they are, with few exceptions, brought up from the bottom in a state of nudity, the unfortunate passengers having been probably drowned in their berths, or before they had time to put on any vestment. It is, I believe, the habit of the lower class of Irish to retire to rest without a nightdress.

At any rate, these corpses had nothing on them; and what appears singular, nearly all the number as yet obtained are females, on whom it is not likely any amount of money would have been found, even had they been clothed. I know not how to account for this circumstance, unless on the supposition that they have been entangled, and held to the spot by the hair, while the men were drifted to a greater distance by the current, or motion of the sea. The seaweed is entwined with the hair of these bodies in a most surprising manner, so that it is found impossible to extricate it.

The people are very particular in dressing the corpses according to their own ideas of propriety, which are, that each must have a shirt, trousers, and jacket, or a chemise, petticoat and gown, as the case may be, with handkerchiefs over the face and feet, and in this array they are interred, without coffins, to make which there are neither materials, time nor workmen. These clothes they have some difficulty in procuring in sufficient number, by raking them from among the wreck at the bottom; and in some instances they assured me they were obliged to furnish them from their own houses. Their particularity as to the number and nature of the garments which they considered indispensable for the dress of the defunct was laughable enough: but, of course, I carefully abstained from any such remark that could reach their ears, and encouraged them to the utmost. They were also exceedingly careful that everyone should be duly interred before sunset, being persuaded that the inhabitants would be nightly visited by the spirits of such as remained above ground.

I have entered into all this detail to explain the foundation of my belief, that the fishermen do not, and cannot, pay themselves, in the way some imagine. Can you give me any assurance that they will be indemnified by the province, or in any other way? Might not the unclaimed proceeds of former wrecks be thus appropriated? The service is surely one of public importance, and one that, but for the good will and exertions of these poor fellows, would not be performed at all. Indeed, there should be more done yet, even supposing they succeed in finishing what they have begun. Their time and means do not allow them to excavate the ground to a sufficient depth. Workmen should be dispatched to form barrows over these hasty sepulchres, or the foxes, and other ravenous creatures, will get at them, and probably tear out the corpses piecemeal.

You will not fail to perceive how advisable it is that some trustworthy person or persons, living near the site of these continual wrecks, should be empowered to take on himself the direction of the necessary proceedings for saving property, interring bodies, &c, and to defray the unavoidable expenses. Even when life is not lost, the plunder of property is often scandalous. You will ask— Would those honest fishermen I found laboring so worthily in the cause of common humanity be so cruel as to pillage the property of the unfortunate sufferers thrown upon their coast? I answer— not impossible, by any means. Those, truly, that were most active in the good work might be least so in the pillage; and some, I doubt not, would be too honest to join at all in such rascality. But you know of what changeable materials men's minds are made. Add to which the habit long established, I believe, on all sea coasts, of looking upon wrecks in the light of a god-send. Nevertheless, I have little doubt that the worst prowlers of this description kept aloof from the troublesome business in which I found the Loran people so laudably engaged.

I cannot give you a better instance of the necessity for some authorized person to be continually on the look-out than what has occurred at Scatari, only about 6 miles from the scene of the Astraea's fate, and but a day or two after it. The barque Fidelity, R. Clarke, master, 183 passengers, besides the crew, from Dublin for Quebec, drifted quietly ashore at her anchors. All landed and wandered three days and nights in the swamps and thickets of Scatari; not knowing where they might be, until nearly exhausted, and three died. All this time, the people of Menadou, close by, knew nothing of what had happened. Not so those a mile or two further along the coast. They had seen a smoke on Scatari; and away they went in search of plunder. They found the ship, of which they took care to say nothing during two days, in which time they secured and secreted the passengers' chests and property, which it is known they are selling privately. There is no magistrate at Menadou, and if there were, he would probably find it impossible to convict the offenders, and still more so to recover the property for the poor passengers, who, in a state of destitution, arrived in Sydney. Now, were there an intelligent active person, whose business it should be to look out for and protect the ships, persons, and property, so constantly coming ashore on the coast, it is evident that many of these iniquitous depredations would be prevented, and many lives saved; and, as before observed, he might be empowered to direct the proceedings and provide the requisite means, in such cases as that I have described at Loran. I suppose our frugal house of assembly would treat such a proposition as a mere chimera, or as a scheme for providing some one with a place if they were expected to grant the funds, but could not an act be passed to make the proceeds of the sale of wrecks available for this purpose? By saving much property, too, such a measure would economize the provincial funds, which, in the present state of things, must often be drawn on, to keep the plundered and destitute passengers from starving, and to convey them to their destination. A lighthouse on Scatari would be another saving on a large scale—but that subject is threadbare.

[The subject of coastal protection may have been "threadbare," but the wreck of the *Astraea* proved the final argument. After 1834, organized assistance was provided for shipwrecked mariners. See **Notes**, pages 132-133.]

The *Astraea*: A Survivor's Letter

NOTHING OF ANY MOMENT occurred until about two o'clock in the morning of Thursday the 8th of May. It was extremely dark, and the vessel was going before the wind under a full press of sail, when the alarm was given. Orders were given immediately to put the ship about, but before this could be effected, she struck upon a rock, which stoved in her bows. In less than two minutes she struck again with still greater violence, which threw her over on her side, with her deck seaward. During the interval, several of the passengers had got upon deck. Of these hapless beings, some were seen on their knees engaged in prayer, holding on by whatever came within their grasp; others were swept off the moment they came on deck. The captain ordered the jolly boat to be lowered, but only a few had got into it when it was dashed to pieces....

I suppose you have seen by the papers the melancholy announcement of the loss of the barque *Astraea*, with all on board, with the exception of three—the carpenter, a seaman, and myself [Dr. Jerome O'Sullivan, ship's doctor]. I will not detain you by detailing the horrors of shipwreck, suffice to say we struck against a rock at two o'clock on Thursday morning, May 8th, and were dashed to pieces in less than twenty minutes. The boy came down to the cabin and shouted out, "There's land ahead!" The captain and I immediately jumped up on deck, half dressed, and were not there more than ten minutes when she struck; the captain at once ordered the boat to be lowered, and I was one of the first that jumped into it. The people on board made towards the boat with the determination that I did. On perceiving this I left it, and got on deck again, foreseeing that so many persons could not get into the boat without sinking it. I was scarcely on deck when the small boat was shattered to pieces. The vessel was now thrown on her beam ends. I then clung to the wheel, got my arms around it, determined to remain there until she struck or went down. I was dreadfully washed by the breakers, the sea was rolling over the entire ship. I now left the wheel, got on the ship's side, and was scarcely there when the wheel was torn off by the sea, and was dashed overboard on the other side. I then saw that the ship was irrevocably lost, and determined to save my life if I could. I plunged off the wreck without further hesitation, and endeavoured to swim to the opposite rock, which I could discover pretty plainly by the foam of the breakers which dashed against it with fury. I gained the cliff unhurt when a beam of timber (torn from the ship) struck me on the back and drove me down the current about forty yards in an opposite direction. However, the returning wave brought me back again, and threw me on the rock on my hands and knees; the timber drifted me off again and dashed me against another rock. I was held under the timber and partly under water for about fifteen minutes, when the beam stuck in the nook of a rock and remained stationary, by which means I was enabled to disengage myself from it and finally, after many exertions, attained the cliff in a state of extreme exhaustion.

I suffered so much then from the cold, that I was going to precipitate myself again into the sea and drown myself at once; but God, in his infinite mercy, ordered otherwise. The two men who were also preserved from the wreck, picked me up in the morning and conducted me to a house, which we found, after about two hours walking, near a mile from the place where we were wrecked. The woman of the house behaved very kind to me—she put me to bed, gave me some hot tea, and also applied hot irons to my feet, which brought me to by degrees. I was next day conveyed to the house of a Mr. McAlpine, where I was kindly treated, and was subsequently brought to Captain Nesby, of the *Brittania*, to Charlotte's Town, my present residence, where the physicians behave very kind to me, having supplied me with money and with clothes. I am hardly able to hold a pen now, I am so weak. I am cut, hacked, and bruised all over, and am afraid you will not be able to read a word of this or make anything of it as I don't really know what I am saying. I should not have attempted to write at all, but to still your fears, by letting you know that I am still alive.

Ever yours, &e.,&e.,&e.,

Jerome R. O'Sullivan

A North Sydney Harbour Tragedy, 1874

by Elva Jackson

In Lakeside Cemetery at North Sydney, just a little to the left of the main entrance, there is a tall monument in the shape of a broken spar crowned with a wreath. One of the first monuments to be erected in this cemetery, it is a memorial to a thrilling and tragic episode in North Sydney's history.

It was the last of November 1874. Capt. James Brown, in charge of the brigantine *G.J. Troop*, laden with coal, was setting out for the West Indies.

With no weather forecasts, Capt. Brown could not know that he was heading for a driving snowstorm with a gale-force wind. His ship soon sprang a leak and he was forced to head back for port; but the brigantine struck near Cranberry Head and he had to drop anchor and hope to be able to ride out the storm.

This ship of his had been unfortunate just the year before. In the great August Gale of 1873, laden with coal, it had been driven ashore at Cow Bay (now Port Morien), and had been badly damaged. When she had been refloated and repaired, she had been bought by the Archibalds of North Sydney.

Now, again, this ship was in great danger. The strong easterly gales increased; and with the huge waves sweeping in from the Atlantic, it appeared that the ship and all on board her were doomed.

When news of their plight arrived at North Sydney there was great consternation. Plans for a rescue were discussed on all sides. Lying in dock at the time was an English bark, the *Mary Jane*. Some of her crew had been members of the Deal lifesaving boats, having been trained at Deal, England, where the boatmen had a reputation for skill and hardihood. These men immediately volun-

23

teered to help take off the crew from the *G.J. Troop*. They were towed down the harbour in a lifeboat to the scene of the disaster; but after a battle of some hours, they were forced to return until the gale would abate.

In the meantime, there were others in North Sydney who were anxious to rescue the men in their desperate situation. In port also was the ship *Peter Maxwell*. A group of men begged to borrow a boat from it. Though Capt. McArthur told them his boats were not of lifeboat dimensions, they refused to be swerved from their purpose.

Thus this boat was launched and it was towed down the harbour to Lloyd's Cove. In the boat were Capt. William Cann, a brother-in-law of Capt. Brown; Capt. Jeremiah Downey of the brigantine *Iris*, anchored in the harbour; Bethel Keenan, sailor and rigger; Capt. Charles Hackett and Capt. Thomas Hackett of North Sydney; and Daniel Campbell of Boularderie. These men all rushed off hurriedly in their great desperation to help their distressed fellow seamen. Those with homes in North Sydney did not even take time to return to their homes before setting out. That morning, Capt. William Cann's wife had reminded her husband again to bring home a fire shovel he had forgotten the day before. As a reminder, she pulled off her wedding ring and slipped it on his finger.

The storm raged as wild as ever with huge waves tossing the frail boat like a cockleshell. As they neared their goal, a huge wave engulfed them and hurled the six men into the sea. The feelings of those on the wreck may be imagined as they watched this rescue boat approach and then saw it capsize before their very eyes. They threw out a line as quickly as possible. It was grasped by Capt. Thomas Hackett, who relinquished it so that his brother, Capt. Charles Hackett, might seize it. Daniel Campbell swam up and seized it too. As another line was thrown, Capt. Thomas Hackett was able to grasp it. Again he gave it up, handing it to Campbell, as he felt that both Campbell and his brother would stand a better chance on separate lines. Bethel Keenan, Capt. William Cann, and Jeremiah Downey had gone down before lines could be thrown. Capt. Thomas Hackett now swam for the ship and, seizing the martingale, held on with both hands until they were numb. Then he took a grip with his teeth as well. Finally he was pulled on board by the crew. Meanwhile, the two men on the lines had been pulled safely aboard.

The bodies of Capt. Cann and Downey were washed ashore at South Bar, a short distance from each other, a few days later. On Cann's hand was his wife's wedding ring. The body of Keenan was never found.

Now the brigantine *G.J. Troop* was in as much danger as ever; but now there were three more aboard. Excitement and anxiety reigned in North Sydney and Sydney Mines. No one was certain about the fate of the rescuers whose boat had been seen to capsize. Most of the people of the two towns gathered at one time or another on the cliffs overlooking the scene while the winds blew and the waves dashed over the doomed ship. At night fires were made along the cliff to warm the watchers and to give light of hope to those on the ship. The day after the disaster, a 24-pound gun was brought to the shore in a vain attempt to shoot a line to the ship.

The ship continued to pound and she was gradually breaking up. On the third day, when her bottom was about gone and her cargo was spilling into the sea, as the crew cut her spars, she worked nearer and nearer the cliffs.

On the fourth day, Capt. George Burchell of Sydney in charge of the *Virgo*, bound from Halifax to Sydney, on approaching the harbour, saw the plight of the wrecked ship. He ordered lifeboats lowered. As the wind was now abating and the waves were slackening, they were able to rescue the crew plus the three would-be-rescuers and take them all to North Sydney.

The vessel broke up and the coal was scattered along the shore only a few miles from where it had been mined.

The citizens of North Sydney in grateful memory subscribed the monument representing the broken spar adorned with a wreath. This you may see in Lakeside Cemetery, North Sydney, with the inscription:

"In Memory of William B. Cann, Bethel Keenan and Jeremiah Downey, who lost their lives on the 1st day of Dec. 1874 in the attempt to rescue the crew of the Brigantine *G.J. Troop* which grounded on Cranberry Head."

The Inquiry into the *Dorcas* and the *Etta Stewart*, 1893

by Michael MacDonald

"Captain Ferguson (of Louisbourg, Cape Breton) was one of Nova Scotia's most heroic sons, who undoubtedly sacrificed his own life and those of his crew in his desperate attempt to save the lives of the utterly helpless men on the barge which he was towing."—*Halifax Herald*, 1893

THE EVENING OF MONDAY, August 21-22, 1993, marked the 100th anniversary of the Great Gale of 1893, one of the most notorious marine storms in the history of Nova Scotia. Often referred to as the "Second August Gale" (in deference to the Great Gale of August 23-24, 1873), the storm of 1893 was both sudden and of enormous force, resulting in substantial damage along the Atlantic seaboard. Over twenty steamers and sailing vessels (and as many large pleasure craft) were sunk or badly damaged between Newfoundland and the New England coastline. The Halifax papers gave it prominent attention in light of the furious intensity of the hurricane along the Nova Scotia coastline.

Late Tuesday evening rumours in Halifax began circulating that a terrible wreck had been discovered on Shut-In Island reef near the entrance to the Three Fathom Harbour. By the time the Wednesday evening papers went to press, it had been confirmed that the steamer *Dorcas* and her tow, the coal barge *Etta Stewart*, had been wrecked during the great gale late Monday night with the apparent loss of all twenty-four crew and passengers.

26

Although obscured by time and overlooked by history, the loss of the *Dorcas* and the *Etta Stewart* was a great sea tragedy in its time. It left an impact on the province as a whole and on two communities in particular—Halifax and Louisbourg.

The pain was assuredly most felt in Louisbourg, then a sleepy pre-industrial village with a population of about 900. Sixteen of the victims were from the port of Louisbourg including the skipper of the *Dorcas*, Capt. Angus Ferguson. In Louisbourg seven women were widowed, and thirty children were left without a father. One woman lost a husband and a brother. Another family lost two sons.

The drama would unfold primarily in Halifax. The Chief Engineer of the *Dorcas*, William Hannah, was a resident (as were the 2nd Engineer and fireman). Chief Hannah was bringing home from a visit to Sydney his pregnant second wife, three children from his first marriage and a 14-year-old girl in his care. His entire family was wiped out.

Front page news across Canada, the fatal voyage would be the subject of an official government inquiry—then a rarely held procedure. The inquiry would focus primarily on Capt. Ferguson's probable course of action during this terrible calamity.

WEDNESDAY, AUGUST 23, 1893:
IS THE STEAMER *DORCAS* WRECKED?

The following letter was delivered to the Halifax Police Station addressed to Chief of Police O'Sullivan:

"Three Fathom Harbour, August 22nd. After the gale, please report that there are 'two or three vessels' lost this morning near the west point of Shut-In Island. I 'presume' it is the steamer *Dorcas*. She lies bottom up. The barge *Etta Stewart* is being broken up. One body has been picked up. Come immediately and take charge."—Geo. H. Graham

Whether the above was correct or not was impossible to verify last night. The driver of the coach which came up from the Eastern Shore last night heard nothing of the wreck.

By Wednesday afternoon however, the contents of the letter had proved to be sadly true. The *Daily Echo* confirmed the reported loss of the vessels and wrote that:

The *Dorcas*, Capt. Angus Ferguson, left Sydney, C.B., on Saturday last with the barge *Etta Stewart* in tow, both coal laden, and had the weather remained fine would have been due here Monday.... The chief engineer of the *Dorcas* is William Hannah, of 14 Moren Street (Halifax). He had on board with him his bride of a few weeks (second wife) and four children.

The *Dorcas* was a 120-ton steamer engaged in the busy coal trade between Sydney, Halifax, and the Gulf ports. Built in Sackville, New Brunswick, in 1888, she initially worked the Bay of Fundy. The *Etta Stewart* was built in Saint John in 1872. This lumbering 787-ton hulk was launched a barque, but was converted to a barge in 1891 when purchased by George E. Franklyn of the Samuel Cunard Company, also principle owner of the *Dorcas*.

Capt. Angus Ferguson was a well-known, highly regarded man around Halifax and the many harbours along the coastal trading route. A native of Louisbourg, he was a product of the large community of Presbyterian (most North Uist) Highlanders that settled much of the greater Louisbourg area of Cape Breton in the early 1800s. While Gaelic was his first language and that of his home, he was educated in English, an important step for those of ambition in the rural Cape Breton of his day.

His desire to be a captain took him to sea at fifteen, and he advanced quickly. After receiving his master's certificate, he served as mate on the *Edgar Stuart*, then for years commanded the *M.A. Starr* out of Liverpool. Then he became skipper of the *Dorcas*. He was a Mason, and although he and his family lived in Cape Breton he was a member of St. John's Lodge in Halifax. In the prime of his life at the age of 45, he had security and status as a captain with Samuel Cunard and Company, plus a good income to provide for his wife, five children and widowed mother.

His friend and Chief Engineer was William Hannah, a native of Greenock, Scotland. He had emigrated first to St. John's, Newfoundland, and then on to Halifax, serving as 2nd Engineer on the Bermuda *S.S. Alpha*. He married a local woman, returning to Newfoundland to begin a family but eventually moving back to Halifax in 1887 with his wife, three children and a teenage girl in his charge, a Miss Lucy Baird.

Mr. Hannah's first wife died in 1891, and he left his Bermuda-based position shortly thereafter to work closer to home and his family. As a fellow member of St. John's Lodge and a good friend, Captain Ferguson was most certainly delighted to welcome him on board the *Dorcas* in 1892 as Chief Engineer.

In 1893 Mr. Hannah raised local eyebrows by marrying the same Lucy Baird who had come and lived with the family since their arrival in Halifax. According to the *Acadian Recorder* of Thursday, August 24, 1893, Miss Baird took charge of the household after the first wife died, and William Hannah married her in February. Their relationship would be described in a cryptic fashion in the early days following the disaster.

The *Recorder* also provided the first eyewitness reports of the scene on Wednesday, August 23rd. Highlighted by the front page headline "A Dreadful Shipwreck—Tug *Dorcas* and coal barge *Etta Stewart* lost with nearly a score of lives!" it continues:

The news is unfortunately confirmed. Mr. J.C. Potts, of the Porter Lake Lumber Company, arrived in town from the scene of the disaster with a report to Messrs. Cunard's office. He says the wreckage was discovered yesterday morning on the shores there, but it was not known what it was. The two vessels were lying there breaking up; one of Mr. Purdy's mill men (John D. McDonald) discovered a broken board with letters on it, "Etta Stewart." Mr. Potts, when told of this remarked, "Poor Capt. Ferguson, the barge must be somewhere."

The seas were running mountain high. About a quarter of a mile to the westward, on Half Island Beach, bodies were seen in the water. Mr. Potts and several others went up. One body was pulled ashore by Mr. Acker and his wife. Mr. Potts recognised it at once as that of Capt. Ferguson of the *Dorcas*; both temples had been smashed in.

During this time six or seven bodies were seen floating in the surf at the same place right underneath the bluff—one a female and a little girl of six or seven years. The others were men. The waves were too high to get them until the tide went out at night.

The body of Wm. Hannah of 14 Moren St., in Halifax had not a mark on it. Mrs. Hannah's body was nude. There were large gold rings on her fingers. Hannah's family had been returning from Sydney. The little girl was his. Where the wreck occurred is supposed to have been on the reef between Shut-In Island and Eastern Passage harbour, about 1 & 1/2 hours sail from Halifax, or 20 miles by the shortest land route.

The first published list of probable victims came from the shipping office of those who boarded in Sydney for Halifax, but whether they were on them at the time they were lost would not be known for a few days. The registered crew of the *Dorcas*:

Angus Ferguson, of C.B., captain.
Hector McDonald, 42, of C.B., mate.
James McDonald, 23, of C.B., able seaman.
William Hannah, 38, of Scotland, chief engineer.
Alfred Tonguay, 36, of Quebec, second engineer.
James Ronan, 29, of Ireland, fireman.
Alex McVicar, 29, of C.B., able seaman.
Norman McKay, 29, of C.B., cook and steward.

On the *Etta Stewart*:

David Baldwin, 44, of C.B., cook and steward.
Edward Kelly, 25, of C.B., able seaman.
Angus McDonald, 39, of C.B., able seaman.
John Kelly, 29, of C.B., able seaman.
M. McAskill, 21, of Louisbourg, able seaman.

All but James Ronan would prove to be included among the victims. All of those from Cape Breton were specifically from the Louisbourg area. But the twelve believed to be on board would double when the first comprehensive report of the wreck was published next day in the Thursday, August 24, 1893, edition of the *Halifax Herald*.

14 BODIES RECOVERED OF THE 24 LOST
IN THE *DORCAS* WRECK

THE *DORCAS* YET TO BE SEEN, BEATEN BY THE SURF, BUT THE BARGE GROUND TO SPLINTERS ON THE ROCK-BOUND SHORE AT LAWRENCETOWN.

No sadder news has been heard in Halifax for many a long day than the loss of the steamer *Dorcas* and the barge *Etta Stewart*, with twenty-four lives. Captain Ferguson was well known in this city, and he was respected as a man and thoroughly trusted as a seaman. The day after Monday night's terrific storm people thought of the *Dorcas* on her way from Sydney to Halifax, but there was no alarm for her safety as it was generally believed Captain Ferguson would make one of the many harbours on the eastern shore. That was the opinion of George

The *Dorcas* and the *Etta Stewart*, 1893

E. Francklyn, who owned this steamer, and when the rumor spread on Tuesday night that the *Dorcas* was lost he reassured himself by concluding that Captain Ferguson had undoubtedly put into Sheet Harbour or some other haven of refuge. BUT HE HAD NOT DONE SO AND HAD MET HIS FATE.

Storms prevailed for three days after Captain Ferguson was ready to leave Sydney. It was not till Saturday the weather looked promising, and he sailed for Halifax, only to run into another and more fearful storm. On Monday a terrible south east gale sprang up which became worse as night wore on, till at last it was a perfect tempest, carrying with it death and destruction. It is likely the Captain believed he could make Halifax by running before the wind or that it was as safe to make the attempt to reach this port as to seek a nearer harbour.

One thing only is definitely known, for not a soul lives to tell the story of the voyage, and that is that the *Dorcas* and her tow, with their brave commander and all his crew were lost when within an hour and a half run of Halifax, at Lawrencetown and Graham's Head. At two o'clock Tuesday morning they were wrecked and all on board drowned, not more than a stone's throw off the cliff lined shores of Lawrencetown. The villagers heard the roar of the storm and feared for its dread consequences, but it was not till next morning they knew of the disaster that occurred almost at their doors.

C. Hudson Smith, who was on the eastern shore on business, returned to the city yesterday, and tells of the sad scene at Lawrencetown. He says: "THE SHORE IS STREWN WITH WRECKAGE splintered into fragments. The timbers look as though ground by some mighty force, the pounding upon the rocks having made the barge little else than a mass of kindling wood." Yesterday when he left there the sea was yet running mountains high, and the surf that beat upon the shore was tremendous.

No one knew what the wreckage was till the bodies were washed ashore, when some of them were identified. Mr. Smith says Henry Acker, of Lawrencetown, was the leader in the work of recovering the bodies. The task was no easy one in the fearful surf. More than once, when a body seemed within reach, it was swept again out to sea, and when the waves brought it back, after several unsuccessful attempts, one after another the bodies were secured till the remains of fourteen human beings had been recovered from the sea. When Mr. Smith left yesterday afternoon eight bodies were lying at Lawrencetown and six at Graham's Head. Many of them were disfigured about the face and head, but there was not as much mutilation as one might have supposed. Their clothing was torn to shreds, and in some cases THE BODIES WERE HALF NAKED.

Henry Acker told Mr. Smith that about 1:30 Tuesday afternoon, himself and wife found the body of a man on the beach. It was large and stout, and was supposed to be the body of Captain Ferguson, of the *Dorcas*. They watched and soon saw two more bodies. About 9 o'clock at night another body was found, and an hour later the bodies of a man and woman were found. Between 11 and 12 o'clock the body of another man was secured. The seven were placed on the floor of Mr. Acker's barn and decently attended to. Yesterday morning the eighth body was recovered and taken in charge by Mr. Acker and those who were assisting him, and another body was seen in the water beyond reach when Mr. Smith left.

The woman found by Mr. Acker had on a plain wedding ring, and a ring with three small stones. On the Captain's body was found a watch stamped, "The Empire, 1889." It had stopped at 2 o'clock.

Six bodies were also found yesterday morning about 7 o'clock at Graham's Head, Three Fathom Harbour. The steamer is to be seen bottom up, but nothing remains of the barge except the wreckage along the shore. THE COFFINS WERE SENT DOWN YESTERDAY, by Undertaker Snow. The body of Captain Ferguson will be brought up and forwarded on Friday morning to Louisbourg for interment. John A. Snow, a nephew of the deceased, will accompany the remains.

Captain Ferguson was one of the most careful and experienced navigators on the coast. Since he was fifteen years of age he has followed the sea, and in all that time he had not lost a life till about a year ago, when a seaman was drowned from the *Dorcas*. He leaves his wife, five children, and a mother and sister, at Louisbourg. James Kelly, a deck hand on the barge, was a brother-in-law of Captain Ferguson. William McGann's family live on Upper Water Street, and are in destitute circumstances. A. Tanguay's widow and one child live in Upper Water Street. Captain Spencer, of Louisbourg, has a brother, bookkeeper at Miller Brothers, Granville Street. The list of victims was not complete and confirmed.

THE LOST: Those on board the steamer *Dorcas* were:

Captain (Angus) Ferguson, of Louisbourg, C.B.; H. (Hector) McDonald, Mate, of Louisbourg, C.B.; James McDonald, A.B., of Louisbourg, C.B. John T. (F.) Sharp, A.B., of Weymouth, N.S. (native to Louisbourg).; Benjamin McRury, Cook, of Louisbourg, C.B.; Alex McVicar, A.B. of Louisbourg, C.B.; William Hannah, Chief Engineer, his wife & three children, (Halifax).; Sadie Musgrave of Sydney, C.B.; A. (Alfred) Tanguay, 2nd Engineer (Halifax, native to Quebec).; D. (David) Kennedy, Fireman, of Louisbourg.; William McGann, Fireman, Halifax.

Those on the barge were:

Captain (Caleb) Spencer of Louisbourg.

William Price, Mate, of Louisbourg, formerly Captain of Schooner *P. Walsh*, P. (Peter) McVicar, George Kelly, James Kelly, A. (Angus) McDonald, Norman McCaskill, seamen of Louisbourg. David Baldwin, Cook, of Louisbourg.

A whole family is swept out of existence in the death of Engineer Hannah, his wife and children. Mr. Hannah had been married a second time, not more than two months, and the family had taken a trip to Cape Breton.... "The last trip the *Dorcas* was here he (Mr. Hannah) had the quinsy very bad, and had partially arranged with another engineer to take his place. But the quinsy grew unexpectedly better, and he resumed his position." The children were spending their vacation at Capt. Ferguson's, Sydney. Mrs. Hannah went there three weeks ago on a visit. The boys have come up several times with their father on the round trip, which took about a fortnight.

The only relative that Mr. Hannah had living, that he knew of, is a stepsister in Scotland. The lost family consisted of:

William Hannah was 40 years old,
Lucy Hannah, 26 years, St. John's, Nfld.,
Mary Hannah, 13 years,
Archibald Hannah, 10 years,
Ewan Hannah, 7 years.

Mr. W.E. Messervey, who lived next door to the family on Moren St., speaks very highly of father, wife and children, and the neighbours sorrow as they would for near relatives suddenly taken away.

By Thursday the disaster was front-page news across the country. The *Toronto Globe* featured the headline: "Seventeen Were Drowned by the Foundering of Two Vessels in Monday's Gale—The *Dorcas* and her Tow Were Wrecked on Shut-In Island

and Wreckage and dead Bodies are Alone Left to tell the Tale." The *New York Times* claimed: "There is no longer any doubt that fully twenty-five people perished in the wreck of the steamer *Dorcas* and the barge *Etta Stewart*."

The *Montreal Gazette* added in its Thursday edition that "the steamer and barge were both unseaworthy. The barge was an old barque with the topmasts taken down." Although standard questions were raised regarding the conditions of the *Dorcas* and her tow at the inquiry, none of the testimony presented by the company was seriously challenged.

The local news was also taking on a combative tone. On Thursday, August 24, 1893, the liberal *Morning Chronicle*, reporting on the recovery of Mrs. Hannah, wrote about her recent marriage and state of advanced pregnancy. The next day the conservative *Halifax Herald* struck out at the *Chronicle*'s coverage. Under the heading "An Unwarranted Slander," the *Herald* wrote:

In the *Chronicle's* desire to be sensational it publishes an outrageous and unwarranted slander upon an innocent woman in its account of the sad loss of the steamer *Dorcas*. The *Chronicle* says: "The body of William Hannah, engineer, who resided at 14 Moren St. had not a mark on it. Mrs. Hannah's body was nude. She was soon to become a mother" and the *Chronicle* adds that Mrs. Hannah was a "bride of a few weeks." The entire family was lost in the steamer, and no relative is left to bring the *Chronicle* to task for the implied slander. Mrs. Hannah's body had about it the remains of her nightdress, which she evidently wore when aroused from her stateroom shortly after midnight when the disaster occurred. Mrs. Hannah was married in February last.

The *Herald*'s action appears to have achieved the desired effect. Subsequent articles regarding the unfortunate Hannah family were silent on the matter.

By Friday twenty bodies had been recovered. John Sharp, Norman McRury, Norman McAskill and, supposedly, Miss Sadie Musgrave were still unaccounted for. It was later determined that the missing girl was actually Mary Hannah, the chief engineer's eldest daughter.

Information was coming together regarding the fatal voyage. The *Herald* reported that the

Dorcas, with her barge in tow, passed Liscomb at 2 o'clock Monday afternoon. She appeared to be working away from the shore. The south-east wind then blowing was on her quarter and aided her progress. It is believed that everything went well until about midnight when being off Three Fathom Harbour the wind suddenly chopped round one point to the southwest, making a treacherous cross sea, which the *Dorcas* could not stem. Every sea would strike her in the teeth and beat her shorewards.

With the powerful engines the steamer had it is conceded that without the barge all would have been well. On the *Etta Stewart*, however, there were precious human souls under Capt. Ferguson's care, and it is presumed he would not cut the tow hawser and leave them to their fate, which was certain death, as the *Etta Stewart* was a ponderous mass of 1200 tons of coal without sail or anything head the winds.

The *Morning Chronicle* added the next day that:

There can be no doubt that the wreck of the steamer *Dorcas* and the barge *Etta Stewart*, accompanied by the loss of twenty-four lives, is the saddest event that has occurred on our coast since the loss of the *Daniel Steinmann* ten years ago. (A large passenger boat that sailed between Nova Scotia and New England in which over 100 people were drowned.) The loss of life on that occasion was considerably greater, but a few were saved to tell the sad tale. In the tragedy at Three Fathom Harbour not a soul was left to give any information as to how the disaster occurred. The storm king had no pity, and his agents, the remorseless waves, cruelly did his bidding and swallowed up the helpless victims, twenty four in number, making sad blanks in many sorrowing homes....

The *Dorcas* lies bottom up on the beach at the head of the harbour, thus being to the east and much more removed from the open sea than the position of the barge. To get into that position the people of the place think the steamer struck on Three Fathom shoal, near the mouth of the harbour, and rolled over into deep water inside and was then carried bottom up to where she now lies partly submerged. All the contents of the *Dorcas*, her boilers, engine, the coal and everything dropped right out of her and carried the deck down also. The copper paint line of the steamer is just at the level of the water.

The *Etta Stewart* is in pieces. Spars and timbers strew the shore. This theory is generally believed, as the bodies of Capt. Ferguson and ten of the crew were found on one portion of the shore, and those of

Capt. Spencer and five of the crew of the barge were found nearly a mile distant....

Joseph Stone (the first Mrs. Hannah was the sister of Mrs. Stone) was seen last evening by a reporter and he seemed very indignant that the bodies of his relatives were not brought to the city. He says he asked to have them brought up, but was informed that the coroner would not allow them to be removed.

The Friday edition of the *Herald* also reported on the burial of the bodies, stating:

It was deemed inadvisable to send the bodies to Halifax for interment by friends here and elsewhere in the province. Coroner Somers was decidedly opposed to permitting a removal of the bodies for sanitary reasons. It was decided, accordingly, to bury them at the scene of the wreck. The Catholics were interred at Chezzetcook, the religious services performed by the parish priest. Captain Ferguson and the other Presbyterians were buried at Three Fathom Harbour, the Presbyterian minister officiating at the graves. [*NOTE: Only one victim, Peter McVicar would remain in this now-forgotten cemetery of Lake Porter— the rest would be exhumed and reburied. The news account continued:*] Captain Spencer, Episcopalian (Anglican), was buried at Seaforth. The graves were carefully marked, so that in case a second interment is desired by friends of the deceased, there will be no difficulty in ascertaining where the remains of each lie.

Regional reaction to the tragedy was becoming available. The Friday *Herald* wrote that in Cape Breton,

It is the talk of the whole county. There is considerable feeling expressed against the introduction of barges into our carrying trade, as our rough coasts make it so dangerous to the lives of seamen. It is the general opinion that legislation should be enacted for the protection of those who follow the calling of the deep. It is impossible to give the readers of the *Herald* an idea of the deep feeling among the people with regard to the loss of Captain Ferguson and his men.

In the same article doubts were raised about the seaworthiness of the *Dorcas*. The *Herald* writes:

Five years ago, says the *Saint John Sun*, the steamer *Dorcas* was on the bay route for a time, and one night she experienced an extremely rough trip. There were about forty passengers on board and several head of cattle, and it was with the greatest difficulty the *Dorcas* was got back to Digby. Few on board that night expected to reach land again. Many people who travelled on the *Dorcas* never thought she was fit to go on an outside (ocean) voyage.

But questions regarding seaworthiness were not pursued.

By Saturday the focus returned to the handling and final resting places of the bodies. Arrangements were finally approved for disinterment if desired by family or friends. The *Acadian Recorder* writes that:

Some of the bodies are to be brought to Halifax. William Snow, of John Snow & Son, leaves again this afternoon for the scene, and will disinter the bodies of Captain Ferguson, William Hannah, his wife and two children and Sadie Musgrave, and bring them to the city for interment. If the body of John Sharp is found it will also be brought to Halifax. Miss Musgrave's remains will be sent by Monday's train to Sydney, C.B., for interment. The funeral of the Hannah family will not take place until Monday at the earliest.

On Monday, August 28th, the *Acadian Recorder* announced the arrival in the city of the five bodies: William Hannah, his wife and two sons and Miss Sadie Musgrave. It continued,

Miss Musgrave's remains were placed in a hermetically sealed coffin and sent on the train this morning with the deceased's father for Sydney, where the interment will take place. Thus goes home the young girl who so gleefully boarded the *Dorcas* last Saturday week for a visit to Halifax, the pleasures of which were eagerly anticipated. She had never been in this city, and it saw her only dead. The bodies of the Hannah family were placed in polished coffins and will be buried tomorrow afternoon.

Alfred Tonguay would also be disinterred and brought for shipment by train from Halifax to Quebec. It was also announced that

The body of John Sharp, fireman of the *Dorcas*, was found (not much disfigured) on Saturday on the shore of Shut-In Island and was immediately interred by Mr. Graham in the Protestant cemetery. It was not identified at the time, but yesterday M.J. Bates (Halifax resident native to Louisbourg) drove down from Halifax, had the grave opened and identified the body as that of Sharp. As he was a Roman Catholic, the body will likely be removed to the Catholic cemetery.

The handling of the bodies became an increasingly sensitive issue. The *Halifax Herald* of Monday, August 28th, added:

Mr. Bates was indignant at the manner in which the body was interred. Neither the clothes nor the boots were removed; nor was the sand removed from the clothing and the body. The remains were placed in a rough square box, covered with an old quilt from the wreck, and only about a foot of earth thrown over the box. The remains will be enclosed in a new casket and taken to the Catholic cemetery at Chezzetcook.

The *Herald* also raised some intriguing questions regarding insurance. It wrote that:

Engineer Hannah had his life insured for $2,000, payable to his wife, who perished in the same disaster with him. The point is this: If she died first he would be her heir, and his family come in for the $2,000; if he died first she would be the heir, and since all the children were drowned her relatives would come in. Which died first? Nobody knows. If we remember rightly, in a case of this kind in an English probate court, it was argued (and perhaps decided) that the presumption was that the man, being the stronger, would survive the longer, being better able to battle against the destroyer's advances.

Reflecting on Capt. Ferguson, the *Herald* pointed out that

He was a member of St. John's lodge (Halifax) and the members of that lodge made arrangements with Undertaker Snow yesterday to have the remains of that heroic man removed from their temporary resting place near the scene of the disaster and sent to his family at Louisbourg.

Captain Ferguson was one of Nova Scotia's most heroic sons, who undoubtedly sacrificed his own life and those of his crew in his desperate attempt to save the lives of the utterly helpless men on the barge which he was towing. There are three bodies yet unrecovered: Malcolm McAskill, of Louisbourg; Norman McRury, of Catalone (near Louisbourg); and the little girl of Engineer Hannah.

On Tuesday, August 29th the *Chronicle* announced that an official inquiry would investigate the disaster under the direction of Captain W.H. Smith, R.N.R., who would be going to the scene to investigate. Another body was found and was identified as that of Norman McRury. Also on Tuesday came the report of the inquest held by Coroner Somers at Three Fathom Harbour on the twenty-one bodies recovered from the sea. The *Herald* published the rendered verdict:

The *Dorcas* and the *Etta Stewart*, 1893

"The deceased came to their death accidentally casually and by misfortune by reason of the wreck and destruction of the steamer *Dorcas* and the barge *Etta Stewart* on the night of the 21st or early morning of the 22nd of Aug. in the vicinity of Shut-In Island near Three Fathom Harbour by which they were suddenly thrown into the sea during a violent gale and tempest and instantly drowned, and not otherwise." It continues by recommending "that this jury call upon the department of marine and fisheries respectfully, but firmly, to place a bell buoy outside Shut-In Island, as it is a place of dangerous shoals in the way of vessels, the scene of many wrecks and cause of much loss of life."

The Tuesday funeral of the Hannah family was covered by all the papers. The *Herald* wrote that:

A sadder sight than the funeral which took place yesterday afternoon is seldom seen. Four of a family were interred at the same time and the only remaining one lies buried in the sand of the Three Fathom Harbour. An immense concourse of people assembled on Cogswell Street to see the funeral.... Mr. and Mrs. Hannah were buried side by side in a double grave, adjoining the grave of Mr. Hannah's first wife. The two children were interred alongside their mother.

The *Daily Echo* wrote that:

The four coffins were placed in one large grave in the southwest portion of the (Camphill) cemetery. The cortege did not arrive at the cemetery until 4:15, but for an hour before that time people began to gather there....

Freemasons preceded the hearse which contained the body of Mr. Hannah. Then followed another hearse with the body of Mrs. Hannah and a third one with the bodies of the two boys. After the coffins had been lowered into the grave Rev. Allan Simpson, pastor of the Park Street Presbyterian Church, held the usual burial ceremony.

Previous to doing so he referred in touching terms to the sad event, the saddest he had ever witnessed in Camp Hill—all the members of a family but one being consigned at the same time to their last resting place. As their pastor he had known them intimately and bore testimony to their sterling worth and christian character. The impressive ceremony of the Masonic ritual followed.

On Thursday, August 31st the bodies were back in the news. The *Daily Echo* wrote that:

The body of Malcolm McAskill was brought up from Three Fathom

Harbour, and will leave on this morning's train for Louisbourg, where it will be interred. There seems to be some indignation about the way the body was interred. As soon as it was found it was placed in a coffin without being washed or looked after in a proper manner. Some parties wanted to wash it, but a man named Graham who had charge of the body, refused to allow them. When the body was interred yesterday it had to be washed, which was not a very pleasant undertaking.

Appeals for assistance were published in the newspapers. H.C.V. Lavatte of Louisbourg wrote,

While the sad loss of the tug *Dorcas* and barge *Etta Stewart* is fresh in the minds of everybody, I would call attention to the fact that at Louisbourg there are seven widows, thirty children and a widowed mother left without any means or sustenance. Our people, unfortunately (through the adverse fishing season), are not able to assist them to any extent, and unless they get assistance from outside I cannot see how they are going to live. Will not some charitably disposed persons in Halifax open a subscription for the relief of these poor sufferers.

The following day the owner of the *Dorcas*, Mr. George Francklyn, opened a subscription for the relief of the widows and orphans. A letter from Rev. J. Fraser Draper (later Archdeacon), rector of St. Bartholomew's Anglican Church in Louisbourg, was published, imploring the people of Halifax to help:

Whenever a really deserving appeal for help is brought before the notice of the general public in Nova Scotia and especially my native town, Halifax, it seldom fails to meet with a willing and generous response. The loss of the steamer *Dorcas* and barge *Etta Stewart* with all hands has, no doubt, evoked universal sympathy. But something more than sympathy is needed by those whose homes have been saddened by this awful calamity.

In nearly every home where the father had been taken away there is actually need for help, and I would most earnestly appeal to a sympathetic and generous giving public to contribute to the relief of those wives and children who are suffering through the wreck of the tow boat and barge. I shall be very glad to undertake any work that may arise in connection with this matter, and perhaps you, sir, might be willing to open up a relief fund in your columns and receive subscriptions for that purpose. If so, I will gladly give $5 and only wish that it could be more.

For weeks the list of contributors was published daily, and the people did prove generous in their response.

On Monday, September 4th, the *Chronicle* announced that the body of Mary Hannah had been found. It seems a group of people from the city had gone to view the wreck site and discovered the body while "dragging through the kelp. It was in a very decomposed condition." She would be the last victim recovered. Norman McRury was never found.

The *Dorcas* Inquiry opened Friday, September 1st, and would deliberate off and on and reach a decision in under a month. Initial testimony was given by Dominion (federal) inspectors of Machinery and Boilers as well as of Hulls and Equipment, both of whom were familiar with the *Dorcas* and testified to her seaworthiness.

On Monday, September 4th, 1893, principal owner George Francklyn corroborated this evidence. Franklyn offered that his firm had

"every confidence in Capt. Ferguson. He had a certificate and was a master of steamboats for several years. We had such great confidence in his sagacity and competence that we did not carry as much insurance on the *Dorcas* as we would have otherwise carried....

"On Wednesday the 16th a heavy gale prevailed at Sydney. Capt. Ferguson was expecting an August blow and I presume he thought this Wednesday gale was the one. He therefore left on the fatal trip confidently. He was thoroughly acquainted with the coast, and knew all the approaches to the harbour. Instructions were issued from the first to him not to leave one harbour unless he thought he could make another.... After leaving Sydney, Saturday morning the 19th, I am informed that the *Dorcas* and *Etta Stewart* put into Louisbourg on Saturday evening, sailed again on Sunday morning...." (Oral history has maintained that an incredible pall came over the town the morning after the sudden storm had passed. The townspeople, so many of whom had flocked joyfully to the waterfront upon the unexpected arrival of the steamer and barge, knew that the sudden and violent storm that swept up the Nova Scotia coast might have caught the *Dorcas* before it made port in Halifax.)

Franklyn states, "My theory of the loss of the vessels is that the captain of the tug boat was making for Halifax, with a fair wind without any indication of a great increase or sudden change being near, when the wind later on without warning chopped to S.W. and blew a hurricane. The vessel not being able to stem it was driven on shore. The fact of the engineer taking his family shows the confidence that officer had in the captain."

Captain Charles Hansen of the steamship *Carroll* was the last known person that saw the ill-fated *Dorcas* and her tow before they were wrecked in the great August storm. He testified:

"Came in sight of the steamer *Dorcas* towing the barge *Etta Stewart*. The position of the *Carroll* was then 5 miles E.S.E. from Egg Island. The other two vessels (since wrecked) were from one to one and a half miles north of us and nearer shore. *Dorcas* was under steam and sail, jibs, foresail and mainsail set. The barge had all sail set, jib, foresail, and mainsail. Their course was westerly or opposite to the direction of my steamer. The sea was rising gradually and it was blowing a good strong breeze from eastward.

"It was squally with thick weather but the *Dorcas* and barge appeared making fair headway. I remarked to my officers that Captain Ferguson would probably harbour at Jeddore. At this time (4:40 p.m.), barometer began falling, but the weather did not have a threatening aspect. Had no apprehension that the barge and steamer were in danger, for I knew the *Dorcas* was strong and a good steamboat. Kept on my course until about 8 p.m. Wind then increased rapidly and barometer fell considerably and the sky assumed an ominous appearance.

"About this time rain poured in torrents accompanied by the peals of thunder and vivid flashes of lightning. At 11 o'clock in the night the wind suddenly hauled to south, and blew a complete hurricane which raised up a cross sea, and caused the *Carroll* to toss wildly. The wind still kept canting to southwest and west during the remainder of the night with unabated force. It rained all night intermittently, with a dense blackness all around which prevented seeing any distance.

"Frequently spoke to my mate during the night about the *Dorcas* and her tow, thinking that if they did not harbor at Jeddore the probability was that the gale had driven them on shore. Only theory I have is that *Dorcas* hung to the *Etta Stewart* until both became doomed. I knew Captain Ferguson, of the *Dorcas*, personally, and knew him to be a good mariner, and well acquainted with our coast. Always heard of him as a cautious man."

Arthur Haines testified that:

The *Dorcas* and the *Etta Stewart*, 1893

"Have been master of wrecked barge *Etta Stewart* frequently. Sailed in her last on August 6th. Was in Sydney when she sailed thence on her fatal voyage about 19th of August. I was to have taken charge of the *Etta Stewart* on that voyage and relieved Captain Spencer who lost his life with the barge at Three Fathom Harbour. As the vessel was detained at Sydney, Captain Spencer was enabled to execute his business and get away with the *Etta Stewart*. I therefore remained behind. Knew Captain Ferguson. He was a skillful and prudent man with whom no one disagreed."

On Saturday, September 18th, Inquiry Commissioner Captain Smith was compelled to postpone his pending decision. The propeller had been found, supposedly with wire and rope wound round it. The new discovery has led some to believe that the loss of the steamer *Dorcas* was due to the propeller becoming disabled by the action of the wire and rope. A piece of stout rope was wound tightly round the broken blades and possibly around the boss. If true, it could suggest that the *Dorcas* had cut free of her tow. Diver Gilkie, however, was positive that the rope was not round the boss but had been washed over the propeller in the strong seas that prevailed for days.

Captain Smith delivered his decision on Thursday, August 28th, 1893. He concluded:

That the master of the *Dorcas*, having been detained at Sydney by a severe gale of wind, on the 18th of August was no doubt led to the belief that it was the annual August gale then blowing and his telegram to the owners that he would remain in port until the gale abated appears to point to the fact that he was a prudent and cautious seaman. As a result of this gale having passed over Sydney, Capt. Ferguson was no doubt inspired with confidence in the weather when starting upon his trip the following day.

In this melancholy catastrophe, the crews of both the wrecked vessels having perished by being drowned, the commissioner is compelled to obtain information in connection with the casualty from other sources.

After taking his departure from Sydney, with the *Etta Stewart* in tow, he called at Louisbourg, which port he left at 9 o'clock on Sunday morning, the 20th of August. At 4:30 P.M. of Monday, the 21st, the two vessels were sighted by the officers of the *U.S.S. Carroll*, that steamer being at the time about five miles E.S.E. magnetic from Egg Island, and the other a little to the north of that position....

The *Dorcas* was observed to be under steam and sail and the barge had all her fore and aft canvas set. The master of the *Carroll* had no apprehension that they were at all in danger, as he had seen the *Dorcas* in pretty rough weather several times before, with her barges in tow, and knew she was a good strong sea boat.... When seen by the *Carroll*, the *Dorcas* with her tow had passed all the principal harbours on the eastern coast where shelter could have been obtained.

With reference to the movement of the barometer at Halifax after noon of the 21st and the following morning, it may be inferred that no indication of an approaching cyclone or gale could have been indicated by the barometer on board the *Dorcas*, up to the time of reaching Egg Island, otherwise Captain Ferguson would probably have gone into some safe place and secured anchorage for the night, when opportunity occurred, which appears to have been his usual custom.

About the time the vessels passed that island no doubt the wind and sea had sensibly increased, but heavy rain and thick weather came on soon after, according to the evidence of the lighthouse keeper at the station, who, however, did not see either these two vessels or the *Carroll* at any time. It is possible that later the master of the *Dorcas* expected that the wind would veer to the S.W., hauled his vessel more off shore to obtain an offing, which may account for the lighthouse keeper not seeing him.

Had he attempted to get into Jeddore Harbour, under the circumstances which then existed, he would have been running a serious risk, as night was coming on and the frequent squalls of rain would probably have prevented those on board from seeing any great distance from the *Dorcas*. From the position the vessels were observed in, near Egg Island, to Shut-In Island Reef where they were stranded, is 24 miles, which could have been made by them in six hours with ordinary weather.

About half past 10 or 11:00 P.M. the wind suddenly shifted to the south and blew with hurricane force, which must have raised a heavy sea and caused the vessels to labour heavily. They were both lying in a dangerous position, between two opposing seas, and would probably have taken large quantities of water on board. It was difficult even for one vessel to take care of herself in such a sea.

The *Dorcas* and the *Etta Stewart*, 1893

The commissioner is of the opinion at this time of great anxiety the two vessels were entirely at the mercy of the waves. The sea broke over them fore and aft and the quantity of water taken on board the barge might have rendered her unmanageable, and as she lost her steerageway every effort that may have been made by the master on the *Dorcas* to keep the vessel up to the sea, they were both driven helplessly towards the coast. The night being dark, the wind howling about the masts and rigging of the vessels, with the terrific sea breaking over them, sweeping the decks with blinding spray, they could have had no possible means of ascertaining the rate of drift to leeward, or the correct position of the steamer. So great was the violence of the wind, it is stated by one of the witnesses that his house shook like a leaf and the sea spray blew over the cliff, 90 ft. in height, at Half Island Point, near the home of the witness, sweeping a thousand feet across the fields. No signals could have been made to the barge from the steamer and even at times during the violent squalls they must have been out of sight of each other.

From all indications it is apparent that Captain Ferguson must have held on to his tow until she was swept towards the breakers at the west end of Shut-In Island. No doubt the knowledge of the fact of his approach to the breakers occurred suddenly and but little warning was given, and when all chance of saving the barge and her crew had been abandoned, and he became conscious of the inevitable danger they were in and the hopelessness of any further exertion being made towards the attainment of his purpose of rescuing the other craft, he endeavoured to sever the wire hawser, with the thought that those on board the steamer might escape with their lives.

Three strokes of an axe made upon the wire hawser, now lying on the shore at East Graham Head, proves conclusively, by the marks upon it, that it must have been struck with an axe, and was actually severed where the cuts were made. The other end, fast to the barge, was probably broken off, as the strands are irregular and appear to have suffered a severe strain.

After having accomplished this it is quite possible that a heavy sea swept over the steamer and put the fires out in the stoke hole and carried the master overboard, as his body was the first to be picked up at Half Island Point, near the former entrance to Porter's Lake, and it was not until several hours afterwards that the bodies of the engineer and

45

his family, with the rest of the crew of the *Dorcas*, were seen floating upon the top of the surf.

Probably many minutes did not elapse before the steamer was stranded. It is supposed by the commissioner she struck first upon her keel aft upon the adjacent reef. The sea must instantly have made a complete breach over her, and being followed by the heavy surf the vessel was no doubt thrown upon her beam ends, and after pounding for a time upon her port side on the rocks (as observed by the planking and timbers being most broke there), she turned keel upwards and was swept in towards the beach.

From the sworn evidence of the diver, Mr. Gilkie, it does not appear that any part of the rope is around the boss of the propeller...and would indicate that the machinery of the steamer was not in motion when the rope became entangled and that the circumstance did not occur previous to but after the stranding of the vessel.

The commissioner is of the opinion that Capt. Angus Ferguson, who lost his life with the others upon this sad occasion, was not to blame for the lamentable result of this disaster. That from his previous conduct and habit it is fair and just to infer that he did not fail to perform the duties imposed upon him in the trying circumstances to avert the calamity. It may be considered by some that it would have been more prudent and wise for the master of the *Dorcas* to have disconnected his steamer from the barge at some safe time before approaching the breakers, in order to enable his vessel to reach off shore and thus have made an effort to save the larger number of people on board the steamer at the sacrifice of the less number on board the barge.

Had Captain Ferguson, however, acted in such a manner and been successful in saving the steamer with those on board, he would have forever been branded as a coward when he reached the land and laid himself open to the serious charge of deliberately and wilfully sacrificing the lives of many human beings for the sake of saving his own. To a brave man this would have been intolerable and it must be acknowledged that in acting as he did he displayed the genuine characteristics of a noble seaman, when, amidst the dangers of such a hurricane and wild sea, he met death at the post of duty.

It is not to be presumed that Captain Ferguson ever gave up all hope of saving the lives of those on board both the vessels up to the very last moment. Had he however severed the wire tow rope at any time before he did and cut himself adrift from the barge, he knew it meant sure and inevitable destruction to every soul on board that vessel.

It is most difficult to realise the grave responsibility resting upon the master of the *Dorcas* at that eventful time, the thoughts impressed upon his mind in such an hour of peril, or the probable influence exercised upon him by the Chief Engineer, whose daughter, with a young girl companion, were on board the barge.

Taking into consideration that the master of the *Dorcas* sacrificed his own life in his endeavour to save those on board the two vessels, due credit must be given to the actions of a courageous seaman, who displayed such heroic fortitude at the time of a most terrible emergency. The vessels were probably wrecked upon the Shut-In Island reef sometime between 11 o'clock P.M. and midnight of the 21st of August.

The commissioner is of the opinion that the loss of these vessels was caused by a furious cyclone which swept over the province of Nova Scotia, and was especially disastrous on the Atlantic coast, on the night of the 21st of August and early morning of the 22nd, but it must be mainly attributed to the very sudden shift of wind from S.E. or S. by W., between half past ten and eleven P.M. of the 21st, and the violent squalls which continued until past midnight of that date, and caused a terrific sea, which drifted the vessels towards the Shut-In Island reefs.

Newspaper coverage ended with the release of the *Dorcas* Inquiry decision.

Most of the twenty-four dead were disinterred and reburied. Captain Ferguson was disinterred twice—once to be buried in Hardwood Hill Cemetery, and again for his final burial in the old family plot at Loch End Cemetery, Catalone, five miles east of Louisbourg.

William Hannah and his family rest under a large granite stone in Camp Hill Cemetery. The dedication reads:

"Erected by the Canadian Marine Engineers Association of Halifax and friends as a token of esteem and regret."

Wreck of the *Ariadne*, Neil's Harbour, 1896

In yet another approach to shipwreck stories, poet Lillian Crewe Walsh tells the following story, a bit of fiction that turns into a personal memoir—a fiction carved from truth that captures not only the events but the feel of the day.

On October 7th, 1896, with a terrible gale blowing, Rev. Robert Atkinson Smith was at a second story window in the rectory at Neil's Harbour—the old rectory that has since been torn down and replaced with a new building very near the same spot. Whether he was writing a sermon or reading or just enjoying a fire on a miserable day is not certain, but he happened to look up and out to sea and noticed a piece of driftwood, a fragment of the mast of some vessel. And he somehow recognized that this was not old wood but wood from a recent wreck and something worth bothering about. He ran outside and got some fishermen, sending them north and south to search for the wreck. The *Ariadne* was located wrecked on MacKinnon's Point. Rev. Smith and some fishermen tried to get to her on foot but it was impossible to get down in that weather. So Rev. Smith dressed in oilskins and hip boots and set out with two fishermen in a dory on that rough sea. They were out 36 hours. They took aboard two survivors and the bodies of three dead men.

Lillian Crewe Walsh in her story below speaks of five men of the *Ariadne* buried at Neil's Harbour. The number is correct. But the dead men were not all found or buried on the same day. From the two survivors Rev. Smith learned and wrote in the record book: "Bark '*Ariadne*' of Chrishana, Capt. Paulsen, from Greenock Scotland, for Bay Vert, Nova Scotia, foundered at North Bay, Ingonish, Cape Breton. Oct. 7th, 1896. Ten lives lost." So the *Ariadne* must have carried twelve men in all. She wrecked on the 7th and the burial service Mrs. Walsh describes actually took place on October 11th, 1896. But at that time only three men were buried: Captain Martin Paulsen, age 50; First Mate Samuel Torkilsen, age 24; Gustav _____, a Russian Seaman of unknown age.

Some time later two more bodies were washed ashore—a Negro cook and another nameless seaman—and these men were buried February 3rd, 1897, bringing the total to five. The plot containing the five graves was fenced in with wood from the wreckage.

The two survivors went home to Norway and told the story of Rev. Robert Atkinson Smith and the people of Neil's Harbour. The King of Norway sent a communion chalice in a fine oak box, as a token of thanks for the kindnesses to the living and the burial of the dead. It was certainly a gift to the people of Neil's Harbour and it is still in use today. It is taken to the homes of anyone who desires communion and cannot attend church. But the communion set (the paten, the chalice and the cruet) was also and singularly a gift to Rev. Smith. And it is the chalice itself that makes us believe that the story of his thirty-six hours on a stormy sea is more than legend—for engraved on the chalice are these words: "Rev. Robert Atkinson Smith, For Aedel Daad"—which means "for a noble deed"— the highest words a monarch of Norway can bestow upon a civilian. And it is a private communion set.

The Wreck of the *Ariadne*

by Lillian Crewe Walsh

WHEN JIMMY opened the porch door he let in a flurry of snow and a cold blast of air. "Never did I see sich a starmy month for this time of year in all my born days," he said as he stamped his feet on the floor. "Over two inches of snow down and blowin a livin gale right in from the Easterd."

"Bad all right," said Dad. "Charles Payne and I went down and hauled the dories up a bit higher, and I brought up the net we got torn up last storm and spread it out on the kitchen loft to dry. We may be able to mend it tomorrow. It won't be a day out fishing, that's for sure."

"No, Skipper," said Jimmy, "it won't be with a terrible sea heavin in and the wind is enough to clip yer." He stopped for a moment. "Do you know, Skipper, a feller from the Cove told me

49

that there's a ship off Phillip Hatcher's point—seemed to be makin poor headway. Spose it be one of those foreign vessels on the way to Sydney or Halifax?"

"That could be," Dad said. "It's kind of late for sailin craft to be round our shores."

Dad seemed uneasy that night and Jimmy did not sing any of the old songs such as "It was the twelfth of March my Boys" or "From Bristol we set sail."

Mother said it was bedtime a bit earlier than usual, but snuggled in a warm bed we forgot the raging storm. We did not know that Dad and Jimmy went to the point to try to get a glimpse of the ship, and that they had not gone to bed when Reuben Payne came down from South Point to tell them a ship was ashore farther up near Green Cove.

The scram box, as Jimmy always called the lunch box, was filled, and Dad and Jimmy and almost all the men went to the scene of the wreck.

It was dark when they came back, wet, cold and tired. The *Ariadne* was a total wreck and heavy seas hindered them from searching for the bodies; but next day the wind had gone down and three men were found and brought down to a warehouse at the shore— and next day two more were recovered. I do not remember if the *Ariadne* carried more than five men, but I do know that was all that was found.

The fishermen from New Haven—the place referred to as the Cove—helped the men of Neil's Harbour to make the caskets. The kindly merchant gave material to cover them. Little pillows covered with white were provided and bits of green spruce boughs were placed on the covers in the form of a cross. It helped take the bare look off the caskets that contained the men of Norway.

Our clergyman was the Rev. Robert Atkinson Smith. I remember the school was closed the day of the funeral, and the little homes of Neil's Harbour had the blinds down as a token for the strangers that would be laid to rest so far from their own dear shores.

John Payne had lit a fire in the little church and the door in the end used only for funerals was opened. The minister looked tired as he waited to see the procession coming over the hill, and when he went to meet them we stood up in the little church.

"'I am the resurrection and the life,' saith the Lord, 'he that believeth on me, though he were dead yet shall he live.'" The burial service had begun.

The Captain's casket came first, then the others were placed two on each side. The little minister spoke of the dangers of the sea. Perhaps because we were children of seafaring men, and well aware of such dangers, the sermon made a lasting impression on us and we were not ashamed of the tears that ran unchecked down our cheeks when he prayed for the widows and children of the men of Norway.

SOMETIMES when I hear that grand old hymn,
"Oh God our help in ages past,
Our hope for years to come"
I see the men of Neil's Harbour standing bareheaded before the open graves. I see the white flag bearing the red cross of St. Andrew's flying half mast, and the surplice of the minister shaken by the breeze. The wind was high now and snow was drifting in little swirls over the brown earth when we left the churchyard.

It was dark when Dad and Jimmy came home that night. The raging storm swept away every vestige of the *Ariadne*. All that remained to remind us of the wreck were the snow covered graves in the little churchyard.

Some months later a very lovely communion chalice was sent to Rev. R. A. Smith by the government of Norway, and a letter to the men thanking them for giving the men of Norway a Christian burial. It was read in the church of St. Andrew's.

The little minister and all the men who took part in the burial service have passed away, but the graves are not forgotten. A neat wooden cross with a picture of a full rigged ship skillfully inserted in the centre marks the graves of the men of Norway.

Wreck of the *Watford* at Schooner Pond, 1932

by Sara MacLean

IT WAS EARLY MORNING, September 10th, 1932—very early morning, about two o'clock. The *S.S. Watford* of Watts, Watts & Co., England, was one of a fleet that included the *Wanstead*, the *Wandover*, and several other coal-burning vessels plying between Sydney and Montreal in ballast. As was the custom of these little colliers, she passed between St. Paul's Island and Cape North on her way to Sydney. Returning laden to Montreal, the ships must travel outside St. Paul's.

It was a mild night for the time of year, and a light wind was coming from the southeast in gentle puffs with calms between them.

By the time the *Watford* was clear of St. Paul's, the wind had strengthened. The barometer was falling alarmingly, and even though the temperature rose even more, a heavy rain began to fall.

The *Watford* was close in on this course, and riding high in ballast. She took the force of the ever-increasing wind on her port quarter. When the duty officer called the captain to the bridge, he ordered increased revolutions from the engine and a little later a change of course to keep her headed more to the east, compensating for the wind drifting her dangerously towards land.

By 5 a.m. there was a heavy sea running, torrents of rain, and the wind had reached nearly 100 m.p.h.

The little collier struggled on, trying to keep boring to the south and east, whilst all the time wind and sea were forcing her towards the coast, always too close to starboard. Sydney harbour was their only refuge, but by the time they came abreast of the entrance it would have been suicide to turn the *Watford*'s head and put her broadside to the sea that was running. The last hope was to try to keep sea-room until they could round the southern head of Morien Bay and slip in behind Scatari Island, there to shelter until the storm was past.

The *Watford* was sound and new. She had only come off the ways four years ago. Her engines were in good condition and there was a large crew, the majority of them in the stokehold, for these coal-burning ships were stoked by hand.

Imagine the pandemonium in that stokehold, the *Watford* rolling and pitching, the heat from the fires, coal sliding in the bunkers, shovels clanging and furnace doors slamming. Down there the stokers would have no idea of conditions on deck. They were shut up below in a hot, dry, dusty hell of their own, full of noise, flames, coal dust, muscles cracking with effort to pitch coal into the boilers, now upwards, now downwards, slipping as the *Watford* struggled on into the hurricane. They understood that as long as they could keep steam up, the ship had a chance of keeping steerageway off the rocks.

It was about this time that Captain Penrid had the wireless operator send off a signal describing their position as "very dangerous."

About mid-morning, she struck. There was a grinding crash and a roar. The whole sea was in an extreme state of turbulence, completely confused and white with foam, the air full of flying spray and pouring rain. Water gushed into No. 2 hold, but on that shoal over the ledge, the *Watford* could not sink, could not even capsize. She was driven farther and farther in, sideways, roaring and grinding over the bottom.

The stokers' work was done forever as far as the *Watford* was concerned. They climbed the ladders to the main deck and stared at the incredible sight. The ship was hard aground, in the very landwash, lashed by towering surf. Everything moveable was being pounded away. On the starboard side a cliff reared up; it seemed almost within arm's length of them. The grinding of the ship's bottom on the rocks, the roar of the waves, the howling wind shut each man off from his fellows as if he had been surrounded by a wall.

Through all this frenzy came the scream of the *Watford*'s whistle, blast after blast, shrieking into the wilderness as long as there was steam to use.

Time seemed to have stopped. They remained soaked and battered by the water, the wind, the unbelievable noise. The stokers, nearly naked as they had been working in the heat below, shook with chill and shock.

The land they could see seemed to all hands an utter wilderness. Remember, most of these people, though not quite all, were city folk, and their contact with the shore at either end of the monotonous plodding journey from Sydney to Montreal and back would be a few hours ashore at either place, where they would see nothing of the country beyond the waterfront, with perhaps a short jaunt ashore to the shops at Whitney Pier in Sydney, the Seamen's Mission hall, or to drink some place near the wharves.

Beetling cliffs streaming with rain and thrashing boughs of the trees they could see ashore seemed almost as threatening as the sea itself—and no one, no one at all, appeared to answer the cry for help from the *Watford*'s siren.

BUT HELP WAS ON ITS WAY nonetheless. Three carloads of men had begun the trip towards the northern head of Morien Bay from Glace Bay and Donkin; but the road across the bar at Schooner Pond was under water, so they had to walk for three miles, heading straight into the hurricane, scrambling up a steep incline, slipping on the wet grass, fighting their way through over a mile of tuckamore, the prostrate spruce forest that grows on headlands where the wind off the sea is so fierce that the trees are unable to grow upright. This stuff is much like walking on a wire bedspring with holes in it. It both supports and impedes the person trying to cross it.

From the south, two more men were working their way around the cliff top from Port Morien.

By the time the rescuers arrived the crew of the *Watford* were trying all means to help themselves. Someone had put off a small skiff. One of the stokers, a big strong man referred to as an African but with the very un-African name of John Johnston, jumped down into the boat as it rolled and plunged between the *Watford* and the cliff. He had a line around his waist, and with all his strength he tried to get control of the bouncing, wallowing skiff.

After hours of work and stress in the stokehold heat and the shock of the outside air on his half-naked body, he collapsed in the small boat, and his shipmates dragged him back on aboard the *Watford*, dead of heart failure.

All this time the hurricane was pounding and pushing the wreck closer and closer against the cliff until there was scarcely the length of a small boat between ship and shore. The surf was breaking and spouting around the *Watford* and up the side of the cliff almost to the top.

But now men were seen ashore, crawling and kneeling on the cliff edge in the storm. The seamen shot a line ashore, and when it had been secured a heavy rope was run out and a rope sling rigged. On this the sailors were brought in one by one, dragged to the top of the cliff and handed into safety by the rescuers. Then the sling was run back again to the ship for the next passenger. It was cruelly hard work, the men ashore could not straighten up against the gale, and were forced to work kneeling or lying flat; and aboard the *Watford* those working at the rope were bruised and half smothered by the waves coming aboard.

As soon as the sailors were brought to land, each with his little bundle of possessions tied to his back, he dropped his pack and fell to helping the rescue crew.

Captain Penrid would have remained with his ship until the last, but he was a small man, and not very young. First Officer Knight and Bosun Murray persuaded him to leave, as they were both young powerful men and better able to handle the heavy rope sling in its trips back and forth between the deck and cliff.

One by one the men were taken off until no one remained aboard except Knight and Murray, with the dead body of John Johnston laid in the deckhouse. The people ashore could see these two debating as to which would be the last to leave. Knight was the older of the two, a married man with a family in the city of Aberdeen in Scotland. The watchers saw that Murray was insisting that he go; they saw Knight step into the chair; they saw him slip and fall between ship and cliff. The surf was gushing in so that at one moment the depth of the water reached nearly to the top of the bank, then on the receding wave the rocks of the bottom were exposed. As Knight fell, the water sucked back, leaving the reef shining bare below; his head struck and he rolled in the incoming surge. Murray left the rope and threw a plank to his friend, but the mate's neck must have been broken, he made no attempt to reach it and was washed away in the sea.

Last man of all to come ashore was Murdo Murray, a native of Stornoway in the Isle of Lewis, northernmost of the Hebrides. A seaman born of a race of seamen, he had striven harder than anyone else to save the ship, to save the lives of its crew, and had seen his shipmate dashed to death almost in arm's reach.

As he was pulled over the edge of the cliff by the eager hands of those on shore his English deserted him and he asked in Gaelic, "*Ann an ainm Dhe, c'ait' am bheil mi?*" "In the name of God, where am I?"

Wet and ragged, the crew were led and helped over the tuckamore thicket, along the cliff edge, down the slope to Ezra Bailey's solitary house at the edge of Schooner Pond, where the Bailey family did everything possible for their comfort until they could be taken away to shelter in Sydney, and back to their homes, and back to the sea again.

The *Watford* lay against the cliff a rusting wreck, stripped of anything useful, with a deep crack from deck to keelson where she had broken on the reefs. Had they been able to round one more headland, the southern head of Morien Bay, she would have come into the shelter of Scatari.

[The news account of the day said that a second mate, Herbert Mante, succeeded in swimming ashore with a line—but the line was carried away from the ship by the storm. He managed to climb the cliff in the gale and joined the rescuers at the cliff edge. Duncan Irvine of Donkin told *Cape Breton's Magazine* that he walked around along the cliff, following the vessel as she came ashore.]

Duncan Irvine, Donkin, remembered:

It was a terrific gale blowing on shore. And there was a mine up here—Dominion Number 6 Colliery—it had closed down around 1925 but a lot of the buildings were here and there was a great big tall smokestack—and the captain of the ship said he saw this stack here and mistook it for a stack in Sydney Harbour.

That morning we saw the ship passing here very close—and we followed down. We expected her to hit a rock down there they

Left, the "broken mast" monument in memory of the *G.J.Troop,* North Sydney, 1874

Above: Saint-Luc de la Corne, survivor and journalist of the shipwreck of the *Auguste,* 1761. Also, his cross of Saint-Louis, which divers recovered from the wreck in the 1970s.

Photo of the wreck of the *Marshall Frank* on the Gabarus shore, 1949. The survivors off the *Marshall Frank* and, right, her Captain, Abe Miles, telling the story.

Rev. Smith of Neil's Harbour and the communion gift he received from the King of Norway

Above: Ralph Rafuse and son, and two photos of the wreck of the *Iceland II* at Fourchu, 1967.

The original wooden marker and (right) the more recent stone monument recalling the wreck of the *Ariadne,* at Neil's Harbour, 1896.

HERE AT REST ARE FIVE CREWMEN OF THE NOREGIAN BARK ARIADNE WHICH SANK OFF THESE SHORES OCTOBER 1 1896

CAPTAIN MARTIN PAULSEN AGE 50 YRS. FIRST MATE SAMUEL TORKILSEN AGE 27 YRS. SEAMAN GUSTAR TWO UNKNOWN SEAMEN

The *SC 709* encased in ice with US seamen trapped onboard, 1943, and rescuers Charlie Bagnell, Ed Levy (left) and Walter Boudreau and a snap of the barquentine *Angelus*.

The lifeboat and some survivors of the *Hurry On,* 1935, and the poet Euphemia Malcolm MacEachern of Judique.

Two of the many graves from the wreck of the *Dorcas* and the *Etta Stewart*–William Hannah and Caleb Spencer.

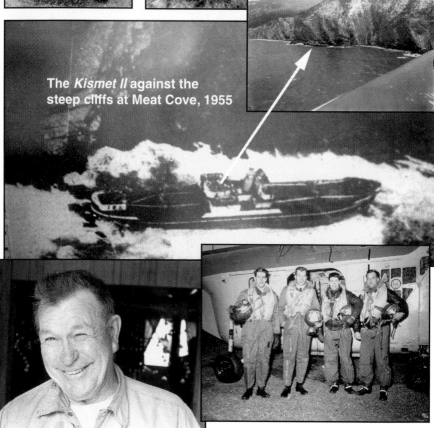

The *Kismet II* against the steep cliffs at Meat Cove, 1955

John Angus Fraser of Meat Cove.

The helicopter rescue crew: Petty Officer Paul Smith; Able Seaman Lawrence Vipond; Lt. Cmdr. Roger Fink, co-pilot; & Lt. Cmdr. Jack Beeman, pilot of the Sikorsky H04S#877

call Schooner Pond Rock, but she missed that. (*You knew she'd wreck?*) Oh, yes, she was in close and she kept blowing her whistle. We followed her around and she came in—and they claim if she'd have been out another 30 or 40 feet she would have made it all right. If she got around that point she had a big channel into Morien Bay and she'd be fairly well sheltered then.

We were walking. Terrific gale. You could try and jump over the bank, I imagine, it would blow you right back on. One of the men had jumped overboard and he got ashore—and I don't know how in the world he ever got up the bank—he was completely exhausted. They shot a line ashore. Then we pulled a big cable ashore and tied it just on some trees. Then they put a bosun's chair on the cable and sent a small line ashore to pull the chair back and forth—and the chair was just a stick suspended from two ropes.

When the man fell, it just happened. You can picture on a day like that, big and heavy gale, spray and everything flying—and then you see him starting to get in the chair—and in an instant he's gone. They found his body round in Morien Bay. Two or three weeks later they found him on Long Beach.

I can remember somebody saying to the captain that the whole gang of them were safe enough on the boat and he said—he was English—he said, "The crew thought they'd be better off on terra firma." But doing that they lost a black fellow and one of the officers.

They were all in there at Ezra Bailey's. Every one of them got a good ducking because the sea was so heavy and you couldn't tighten the line—we only tied it to scrub—no big solid trees around there—couldn't tighten it anymore than they dare, and the weight of a person going on, they went right down into the sea.

Martha Bailey, Schooner Pond, remembered:

I can remember all the men coming here. We were in the kitchen. We were chased out of the kitchen into the dining room, out of the dining room into the bedroom, from the bedroom upstairs. You know, as they were coming. They were wet and frozen, standing by the stove. It was a bad day—oh, yeah—the front door blew in and windows were blown in. And as they were coming in, they had a gallon of rum on the table—and as they came in my mother gave them hot rum and dry clothes and put them in beds, the ones that wanted to go....

I remember my brother taking me on board. They cut a little piece out of the bottom of the boat later, but I remember a rope ladder up the boat and halfway up there were wooden steps and he took us up that—and I remember I was terrified. After that there were people start coming and cut it up and took it away with trucks. But I was only aboard once—my father wouldn't let us. He was Ezra Bailey. (*He was one of the first men at the cliff edge.*) We were sitting having breakfast and we saw Gussy MacIsaac— he was a neighbour; he's dead now—he came by here and he came back and he said, "There's a boat in, Bailey." Then he went down and he got Mack Borden—and the three of them went to the cliff....

Sid Simons from Halifax bought the wreck but it was here a long time, really. First, Standard Pavement Company was hired to cut her up and take her—that must have been in the thirties. They were taking it and loading it on boxcars at Number 6 and sending it to the steel plant and other places. Between 1945 and 1950 is when they took the last of it. That's when the boilers went.

Shipwrecks on the Fourchu-Framboise Coast, 1912-67

These stories came from conversations along the easternmost coast of Cape Breton, with Malcolm MacDonald of Fourchu as the guide. I was looking for stories for *Cape Breton's Magazine*, and we travelled from home to home, one story pointing us to the next. The days were wet and cold and dreary and yet the welcome and sharing made them warm, comfortable and, in memory, cheery. These stories stay alive as people continue to tell them to one another, and welcome any excuse to sit back, share tea, and tell them again.

Wreck of the *Mikado*, 1924

ARTHUR SEVERANCE, Fourchu: It was a beam trawler, the *Mikado* [wrecked May 1924]. It's a Japanese name. (*Was it a Japanese ship?*) No, no. English. One of the earlier beam trawlers. She was on charter—I suppose it'd be the National Fish Company in its earlier days. They probably did have more than one beam trawler on charter, but this one, her charter was up anyway, and she was going to go back to England. They were on their way from Canso to Louisbourg for bunker. They used to bunker a lot of ships at Louisbourg then. They had a coal pier there, and they used to ship coal from there, too, for export. And she was bound there for bunker. Oh, I guess there'd been a bit of partying, according to one of the survivors. Somebody wasn't doing his job, and she was wrecked on Winging Point, Framboise Winging Point Rock, right on the—well, it's sort of a natural breakwater. Fishermen had shanties there years ago. In fact, my

59

father fished out of there for quite a while, in the days when the lobster fishing was all done with rowboats.

This beam trawler, she didn't hit the rocks. She struck a breaker at the eastern end of the rock. It was early in May, but it wasn't what you'd call really bad weather. There was some haze and fog, but there had been quite a heavy blow a few days before that, and there was a ground swell running. You know what I mean now, a big sea—not lop, but a heavy ground swell. And just after she struck—she was a small steamship—they were blowing the whistle. We heard this whistle blowing, got up, and walked up the shore. We got up there, well, you could hear the hollering, calling—some of them had got up in the rigging. But before daylight, we had picked up five bodies, washed ashore. Most of them at the western end of the rock. Came around into a cove there called Harriet Cove. Well, that was named after another ship that was wrecked there, the *Harriet*, a sailing vessel.

So they picked these bodies up and they brought them over and put them in a shanty that my father had there for years. I think there were seventeen in the crew—and there were twelve of the crew got in the rigging on the foremast. She was heavy shrouds and rattlings, and they went up the rattlings as far as they could get. And there were five, I guess, that got on the bridge. But the sea was so heavy, it just carried part of the superstructure away. The bridge went, and the men that were on it went with it. Well, those were the bodies that we picked up there in the morning.

After daylight, you could see the vessel quite plainly. And the fog lit up, you see. Someone had come back here to Fourchu, and where the wife lived down here—MacLeans—they had a telegraph office there—there were no phones in those days here. And they sent a message. They told them that this ship was wrecked on Winging Point. So they dispatched a tug, the *Ocean Eagle*, she came up. But there's another Winging Point. And there was just Winging Point, that they telegraphed, where the vessel was wrecked. I guess the *Ocean Eagle* spent at least four hours, searching around in the wrong area, looking.

Now in the meantime, they got a dory off the beach up at Framboise Winging Point. There were a lot of people had gathered up there by that time. For the area here, I'd say 25 or 30, that would be from the community, maybe more, but there'd be at least that many. They were trying to get a line out to her, see. And she was far enough off—she'd be about 150 yards from the shore, right off the beach. She had hove in a bit with the heavy seas—I suppose she wasn't quite that far then. She had got right on top of the breaker, or in between the two of them, I think. But when those seas would strike, you wouldn't see the men in the spar at all. The spray would fly. So anyway, they got the dory off. There were two or three other boats there, too—big, we call them, flats or stemmers. But they launched the dory.

There was a MacKinnon, Herbert MacKinnon, attempted for to put a line aboard of her. And before he went there, now, there was my cousin, Wilbur Severance, he decided he was going to try to shoot a line across. He had a big muzzleloader, made a line fast in the end of the ramrod, put a tremendous charge of black powder into it. And he was a big heavy man, anyway. He put that against his shoulder, and—he didn't want to fire straight towards the spar, where the men were in the rigging, but tried to get it so it would come fairly handy, you know. And be goldarned, he put the line across her. It was, I suppose, about ten feet from the chain plates— that's where your shrouds fasten in, at the gunwales like, or at the bulwarks. And there was one fellow went down, tried to get to the line, and this heavy sea hove in, and he hung onto the rattlings at the bottom. When it went by, before he got to get that small line which you'd use to pull a bigger line out, that cut off on the steel rail.

So then this fellow [Herbert MacKinnon] got out, tried to go with the dory—one man, tried to get out a heaving line aboard. Well, they knew when he got close enough to the vessel, to the ship, to put a heaving line on, that he wouldn't be able to do anything to get back. So they had a rope—I'd say it'd probably be about one quarter inch, manila rope—long, long line, fast to the dory, so that someone on the shore, if he got in difficulties and couldn't row out of it, that they could pull him in to where he could use the oars again. So he got out there, and he made several attempts to put the heaving line aboard the ship. But every time that he got in position, there'd always be a heavy sea come in and swing him back. So they finally had to give it up.

Well then one fellow, one of the crew, a big able fellow, a

fine-looking man too—he had a lifebelt on, he came down off the rigging, and when the sea was running in he made a dive into it. Figured he was going to come in with the sea and swim ashore. But what he didn't know, the position they were in, where the wreck was located, it was not exactly a whirlpool, but you could only go so far and the suction would haul you back. And he drowned in the surf there. And a strong swimmer, too. He didn't go under—just the surf—he couldn't get air, couldn't breathe air. When that heavy sea would strike, the foam and all, he was into a continuous blanket of foam. He couldn't hold his breath long enough for to get his lungs filled with air again. And he couldn't get away from the ship. The current or tide—more a current than tide—around the ship was holding him there, and he couldn't get away. He'd go so far, the body'd go so far, and come back. Well then, his body drifted away, and it went up around the western end of the rock and came into the same place where we had picked up the five in the morning, before daylight.

Well, the *Ocean Eagle* got up there along mid-afternoon. There were still eleven men in the rigging. There wasn't anything of a breeze to make a bad lop, it was just more or less of a gentle breeze; but this thundering great big swell was still coming in, heaving in there. And she laid off outside the rock there. They got a lifeboat over. I think there was—I'm not sure now—I think it was four men and one of the officers in the lifeboat. Four men on the oars, I think. They started pouring oil overboard from the tug. And as that oil worked in, it got into the ship, and the heavy sea would come in but it wouldn't break. The surface of the water—[the oil] was keeping that sort of smooth. Not calming the swell, but just the surface of the water, that you didn't get that breaking action. When the water peaked up, it wouldn't break, it just kept on going smoothly. And they came in with the lifeboat, pretty nearly directly under the top of the spar, the masthead of that spar where she was leaning out. Like the ship was parallel to the shore here, and then she was leaning out from the shore. They came in almost directly under the masthead. And there was a line dangling down—it was probably a halyard of some kind that belonged to the rigging. They were going to throw a heaving line up to the spar, but a fellow that was right on the top, he grabbed onto this halyard and he slid down into the water. And they threw the heaving line to him. He grabbed it and they pulled him aboard the lifeboat. Then they did that one after the other till they took ten men off.

One man died in the rigging, he was dead in the rigging. Naturally, they couldn't handle him anyway, to get him in, and they left him there.

I'm not sure just how many they took the first time. There was a big lobster smack here. A man by the name of Alex Ferguson was on the smack. She belonged to the cannery that operated down here then. He was up there. He came part way in towards the lifeboat, and they transferred whatever number of men they had aboard the lifeboat—I think it was six or seven. Then he ran back outside, and the lifeboat went in and got the remainder of the men that were able. So Ferguson came in here, and they took the men off the smack. One of the crew stayed with us; people around would take one or two of the fellows in their homes, kept them until they went.

There wasn't much more than an hour after the men were taken off that spar, when the spar collapsed. Whether the weight of the men on the rigging was holding it there, you know, helping to keep the spar there, or not—it'd be just anybody's guess. They were up in that spar from I'd say probably between twelve and one o'clock in the morning until around two or half past two in the afternoon, or maybe three—about three when the last probably was taken off.

That's the only one that I saw where there was a loss of life involved. And not able to do anything.

Wreck of the *Iceland II*, 1967

ARTHUR SEVERANCE: I've never seen a shipwreck at the actual time it happened, or that sort of thing. I've seen one just a day or two after it happened. That one was out here [a portion is still on the shore], the *Iceland II*. She was from Prince Edward Island. They came in—they were in a southeast snowstorm. She had two captains—one was a qualified navigator, the other was acting captain. He was more of a, say, fishing expert. A good fisherman and so on. But I don't imagine that he was trained too well in the use of navigation equipment. The navigating captain—her regular captain—was ashore.

It's not so many years ago, sometime in the late '60s. **Sara Severance:** She was ashore for two days before anybody found her. It was a storm, you know, and nobody went out. **Arthur:** Terrific snowstorm. It was in the winter, a southeaster. There were two of these stern trawlers that were fishing in the same general area, started in. Well, this one was supposed to be heading for Louisbourg, and the other one was going up to the States. Well, the other one made port all right, but this one was coming in on just automatic pilot. And the first thing that I guess anyone was aware of—there were no survivors, no one to find out exactly what happened—but she struck right into the bluff rocks, right back here, just east of Bear Cove. Hooper's beach—yeah, it was the old Hooper property, right on the back of that. There's bits of her out there yet, up on the bank where the sea fired it up. It was in February—in that kind of weather, nobody would be going out. **Sara:** Two young boys were out there for a walk, the MacKay boys, and one sighted the wreck. **Arthur:** I think they only got one of the men aboard the ship. He was in the wheelhouse, frozen stiff. I think they got all the bodies, though. Along the shore. But they were quite a few days before they did recover them. No survivors.

RALPH RAFUSE, Fourchu: (*Was the* Iceland II *a vessel that was around here before?*) No. I never heard of her, that's the first time I heard of her. (*How was she found?*) Well, it was Brian MacKay, he walked up the beach—it was him that saw her—she had been there a day or so—I don't know how long. But I know I was down aboard my boat here in the harbour just a day before that. I could smell fuel oil and I could see pieces of styrofoam floating around—that's the stuff that had blown over the hill, that had come out of her. I never thought anything of it, but it was that day that he found her, sometime through the day.

She could have gone in through the night. I heard a fellow saying that he thought he had heard an engine running through the night out back there, but I don't know if it was that or not. (*This is February 24, 1967. What kind of weather was it?*) Well, the day before that, it was blowing a southeaster—oh, I guess it must have been blowing 115 anyway, I would say—a southeaster, and snow. And then that's how come I went aboard the boat the next day. There was no wind the next day, and I went down to see if my boat was all right—she was tied to the government wharf. (*A southeaster....*) That's just about one of the worst ones on this shore. It's the worst, I guess, you can get here. It was a snowstorm.

I found out through the day. I was up there then, once I found out she was ashore. It was an awful sea on. As soon as people heard about it, they started coming. There wasn't too much of anything to see—only pieces of dories and pieces of stuff that was broke off of her, you know, that had got torn off. But there was no way you could get aboard of her—you couldn't get aboard of her that day at all. (*She wasn't right in to the shore, was she?*) No, she wasn't, she was off a little piece, not too far. You could throw a stone to her, but you couldn't get to her. You couldn't even walk out to the edge, because the sea was coming in, mountains of sea then. Pieces of dories, and pieces of wood coming out of her from different places of her—down in the hatches. And the styrofoam that was coming ashore, that was insulation that was down the fish hatches.

She was a stern dragger. She had been into Louisbourg, so I hear, and she had got fuel—that was a couple of days before she went ashore. She had left for back out to the fishing grounds. And I guess they heard that the storm had started, and she was supposed to be on her way back in. And they figure she was supposed to be heading for Louisbourg really—either Louisbourg or Mulgrave—and here's where she landed.

I got the charts off of her, and one of the charts was marked out for Fourchu Harbour. Now, if that had been marked before they left out there, or was that marked from some other time? She might have figured it was the shortest place to come in. Although it's one of the worst harbours, you know, in a gale of wind like that. And she could have tried to come in here. It was set for automatic pilot, in the wheelhouse. But the sea could have put that thing over on auto, for all I know. But I know the lever was set for automatic. So they could have figured it was going to take them so many hours to come in, and set her on automatic pilot, and I guess it was closer than what they figured it. Then she had the wind behind her, too, helping her along. So they could have run an extra 10 miles faster and fetched up here.

(*When you were on the shore, were you aware of the crew?*) No. Well, we had a pretty good idea about the crew, without there was somebody down inside alive. But the sea that was on, there was no way that anybody'd survive coming out of her, because they'd just get beat to pieces as soon as they left the boat, they'd get beat up—there's no way that they'd come ashore alive. It was just about impossible. There could have been somebody alive inside. (*But you weren't hearing anything?*) No. Well you wouldn't, there was too much of a roar from the sea. You wouldn't hear anybody without they were—I don't know, if they could fire a gun or something you might hear it—but you wouldn't hear anybody down inside of her.

But if they would have stayed inside of her, they would have lived. Down in the front compartment. They would have survived. Because a day or so after that, when it calmed down that I could get aboard, I swam out to her, and I got aboard of her. And I was down into her. And the clothes were dry, down into the lockers. So the sea was going over the back part of her. You see, they didn't know what was going on, I guess, and according as they came up from down below, they were washed overboard and that was the end of them. Because if the clothes stayed dry down below, the men would have survived. Because she couldn't go down any further than she was. She was already on the bottom.

(*If only they had realized that, and hadn't taken to the dories.*) Oh, I don't think they even got near the dories. Those dories got beat apart as soon as that thing went in there. They just beat to pieces. Just as soon as she struck, the sea just smashed everything that was on her to smithereens, and drove it off of her. And as soon as they came up or went out, they got washed off of her, and that was the end of that. The only thing—down in the front section of her, it was watertight. It was just the same as you were in a big tank. It could break over it all it wanted, and the water wasn't going down. Because the stuff was dry. As soon as you came out, that was it. Sticking your head out was just the same as walking out in front of a machine gun.

There was only one fellow that was found aboard—the Coast

Guard took him off—he was frozen to the ladder—that was down on the stern section. He had been, I dare say, down in the engine room when she struck the rocks, and he started trying to come up. There was so much sea probably, coming down from up above, because it smashed all the windows out of her, all the back windows and everything were smashed out. And I guess he just froze. He couldn't get up and he couldn't go back down—he froze there. I guess he just held on at a death grip—that's about the size of it. And then he froze there.

See, once the sea calmed down a little bit, that there wasn't a continuous pour of water coming down there, then it was cold, and he froze there. He just froze there. Because you take the steering wheel. I took the steering wheel off of her. But now that steering wheel wasn't standing up where you'd be steering the boat. I found that underwater ten feet from where it's supposed to be. It was torn right off, just ripped right off—the steering wheel, the steering post, the whole bloody thing was just torn right off. Windows were all gone out of the back, where the sea was hitting her from behind, the windows were gone. The radar up on the roof of her, that was torn off. That took something, to tear that off.

The Coast Guard sent a helicopter out. It was the next day, I guess it was. They took the man—the body—off of the boat with a wire. They ran a wire from the wheelhouse of the stern section of her to the shore. And they strapped him on the wire, and they took him in that way. I think he was partly dressed. Some of the clothes could have been torn off him trying to get him off the ladder.

That's the only one that was on the boat. There were nine missing. (*Did they ever find the nine?*) Not really. Parts of all nine. But not to say that they found a whole man, no. Because the next—even, oh, I guess it was a year afterward—they were still finding pieces of bones that were coming out of the beach or somewhere—I don't know where it was coming from—it was just showing up on top of the gravel. (*So a whole man was never found after that?*) Not really—there were parts that were missing, yes. They'd find a jawbone out of a man, or a piece of a head, stuff like that, for a year afterwards, I would say.

I think it was a day or so after that, they found a fellow at the breakwater. And I think it was a day or so after that, they found a couple down around Belfry, somewhere along the line down there. Then they went to work and they got a front-end loader out at Bear Cove digging the beach up, see what they could find, you know, figured they might have been buried in the gravel. They never found anything then.

(*What finally happened to the* Iceland II*?*) First, the stern section, it just got beat off. The bow section was there for the longest time, and then that got driven ashore a piece to the west of where she had gone ashore. Just a little bit of her left now—she's pretty well beat up. There was very little salvage done to that, very little that was salvaged on her. No fish in her when she came in—she came in light. When she left to go up to the fishing grounds, if she ever reached all the way out there, I don't know. But she didn't fish when she got there, because there were no fish come in into her. Just nothing but a total loss.

Wreck of the *Thordoc,* 1940

ARTHUR SEVERANCE: One more ship that was wrecked at Winging Point, the *Thordoc.* (*In March, 1940.*) **Sara Severance:** Oh yeah, that was my ship. **Arthur:** She fed the most of the crew for a few days. **Sara:** It was on a Saturday, and I was baking—oh, I did an awful lot of baking—it was only the four of us, him and me and his father and the son. I did an awful lot of baking, an awful lot of cooking—and I wasn't expecting anybody. His father said to me, "Oh, well now, you're okay, you won't have to do any cooking for a whole week or more." I said, "No, and I'm glad of that." So I had everything all set. I had a great big crock of beans cooked, a great big jug of corned beef, and pies, and everything you could think of. That night about six o'clock there was a rap came to the door. And there were seven men. They were wrecked out here. I had to take them in, some of them I had to give them dry clothes—they were wet, and they were hungry—were they ever hungry! Oh gracious alive, I just had enough to feed them for supper. Then I had to find beds for them, make them comfortable for the night. And I had them for five days. But they were an awful good bunch of men. They used to help me wash the dishes, clear the table, set the table, bring the coal up from the basement. (I guess they were glad to be alive.) I guess they were.

Arthur: She was an old upper laker—not the real big ones, now—but these used to come down in the old days. This old *Thorduc*. She was getting pretty ripe, anyway. We always suspected they were looking for a good safe resting place for her. And she found it, right alongside of the Winging Point Rock. The smoothest weather—of course, foggy, thick fog. They must have had some pretty good navigation for to land her in there that day. All they had to do was put a gangplank from the ship to the rock and walk ashore, walk to the rock. **Sara:** I have the stool that the captain was sitting on, from the wheelhouse—he brought it down to me as a souvenir. I had the cook, and he said to me, "You wait," he said, "I'm going to get up to the ship. I know where there's a lot of food," he said, "I'll bring it down." He went up, and he brought a pan with a lovely meat loaf in it. I still have that pan, and I bake bread in it.

Arthur: She was supposed to be coming down to Louisbourg. She had made a few trips carrying coal from Louisbourg up to Halifax. She did her part in the Second World War, I guess. The old ship was cut up. Scrap metal—most of her was hauled in out from Winging Point, and trucked in—probably in to the steel plant. She was recycled, anyway.

Wreck of the *John Harvey,* 1912

JOHN HARDY, Gabarus: You know, the *John Harvey*, she went ashore in January 1912. And she went to the head of Winging Point Beach [near Gabarus], on those rocks up there. And one fellow, what was his name, Edith? **Edith Hardy:** John Foote. **John:** He went ashore with a rope. **Edith** [singing]: "Then young John Foote a rope he took." **John:** He took a rope ashore. **Edith:** Tied it around his waist. And of course it went from the vessel. And he swam. **John:** And it was in the wintertime, too. And cold. Very cold. And the other fellows all got ashore. **Edith:**

They all went ashore on that rope. The last fellow got kind of tangled up.

John: So then they started to look for a place, for shelter. And they went down toward the Winging Point—there were camps down there at that time—fishing camps. And those fellows—Captain Kearly and the mate was Bill and the other fellow—well, they got into camp. This fellow who took the rope ashore and the last man that came ashore—they lay on the beach. And they died there. The other fellows started for Gull Cove. They didn't know where they were going, of course. And my father met them out on the beaches.

When they found them, they were carrying a bird, an old sea bird, so they'd have something to eat. And they were that weak, my father said when the captain would put his leg down in the snow—my father would have to pull up on his leg. And he got him to a house down on Gabarus Cape, Henry Bagnell's. And they got something to eat. And they came into Gull Cove afterwards.

And the first fellow that left the ship, he died, and the last fellow. And I was there and saw them before they ever went off of the beach. One fellow had a chew of tobacco in his mouth. And they were no further from the camp than I would say from here over the harbour—right close there. Why the other fellows didn't go and get them I don't know. Perhaps they were too far gone to go and tell them that they had found shelter.

(*Did you see the wreck itself?*) I saw a piece of it. Nice-looking ship, painted white—three-master. If they'd have stayed aboard in the forecastle, they would have been drove right in over the rocks. They'd've been all right. But the other went to pieces. And all this stuff came ashore on the beaches—rubber boots and everything, just cargo. Loaded.

BERT HARDY, Gabarus: The *John Harvey* left Gloucester, general cargo, bound down on St. Pierre. That was her destination. She may have had other ports o' call in Newfoundland as well. But it was a southeast gale—worst storm of the whole year—and he got down off Scatari. And there's a shoal on the eastern end of Scatari called Hay Island Shoal. And it runs off there for maybe a couple of miles. Very shallow water, and breaks quite heavy in a storm, and he was afraid he wasn't going to clear Hay Island Shoal. And he tacked and stood back to the west'ard. And when he ran back, he made this buoy. But he couldn't tell what buoy it was. It was all iced up. It was Guyon Island Buoy. He took it for Louisbourg Buoy. But he didn't see Louisbourg at all. He came up outside of it. And she went in between Guyon Island and the Big Shoal. And she struck up at the head of the beach. She cleared all the other shoals, went right in and struck shallow water at the head of the beach. On the 9th day of January, 1912. And by the time she reached the beach, he told me she was cleaned right off to the waterline—the bottom had gone right out of her. When she hit she turned broadside and drove in with the sea.

The Wreck of the *John Harvey*, or, the Belleoram Boy
by Lillian Crewe Walsh

You people that work on the shore, how can you understand
The perils of the ocean, when you are safe on land?
But many a brave young sailor lad for adventure's sake has roamed,
To follow the fortunes of the sea, far away from their native home.

And many a man from Newfoundland, when the winter winds do roar,
Has been in coasting vessels near the rough Cape Breton shore.
In January 1912, Captain Kearly did command
The schooner by name *John Harvey* from Belleoram, Newfoundland.

The wind a gale from the southeast blew, the worst storm of the year;
The *John Harvey* sailed from Gloucester, bound for the Isle St. Pierre.
She was loaded with general cargo, and loud the winds did roar,
When on the tenth of January the *John Harvey* went ashore.

The Captain gave orders to his crew, the vessel to dismast.
The boats were frozen on the deck, the sea swept fore and aft,
Said Captain Kearly to his men, "My boys it is no use,
I'm afraid that we are doomed to die near the shore of Gabarus."

Then young John Foote, a rope he took and tied around his waist,
Said he would swim for the nearest land, and the icy foam he faced.
Oh! Bitterly cold was the winter's night, the seas rolled mountains high.
And tossed and battered by the waves was the brave Belleoram boy.

The wind it blew a hurricane, and the night was bitterly cold,
It chilled the heart of the sailor lad, a hero young and bold.
And bruised and battered by the sea, he at last the shore did reach,
And with his badly frozen hands made the rope fast on the beach.

The crew of the *Harvey* got ashore, there were six of them all told.
They owe their lives to God above and the sailor boy so bold.

71

But Keeping and the brave young lad, by exhaustion overcome,
Died near the shore near Gabarus far from their native home.

John Keeping and this brave young Foote, they laid them down to rest,
Each thought of his native home and the ones they loved best.
They knew that death was drawing nigh and in the prime of youth
They gave up the struggle for their lives, near the shores of Gabarus.

The survivors walked to some fishing shacks that stood upon the shore,
Much hampered by their heavy boots and "oil skins" that they wore.
They had no match to light a fire, how awful was their plight
And their struggle for existence on that stormy winter's night.

But help soon came from Gabarus and to them the tale was told
Of the loss of the *John Harvey* and the Belleoram Boy so bold.
God's blessing rest upon them, they did all that they could do,
To comfort and aid the survivors of the *Harvey*'s shipwrecked crew.

Captain Kearly and his hardy crew, a sad disheartened band,
With the bodies of their comrades went back to Newfoundland.
As they followed the caskets to the train, the tears fell from their eyes
As they thought of the friends in Newfoundland of the brave Belleoram boys.

Good people of Belleoram, with you we sympathize,
Don't fret or mourn for those brave boys, for Heaven was their prize.
And all ye bold young sailor lads, think of this noble youth,
Who died far away from his native land near the shores of Gabarus.

Wreck of the *Marshall Frank*, 1949

DAN NORMAN MACLEOD, Framboise:
Aw, it was a pretty cold winter. It was pretty cold weather at the time the *Marshal Frank* was on [February, 1949]. But the day it happened, it was a fine day, beautiful day. And I was shoeing the horse in the garage—it was one shoe that had come off on her—I was hauling pulp—there was someone walked in. How many came to the house, was it three or four? **Mrs. MacLeod:** I think there were five, gave them breakfast. Dan Norman: And they never said a word. Said, "That's a fine-looking horse you've got there," you know, they seemed so unconcerned. I said, "Where did you come from?" "We're shipwrecked," he said. "We're shipwrecked." They told me it was up the shore. They'd come up the lake, you know, up the cove.

They hit a reef. And they abandoned ship. The captain wanted them all to abandon ship. But there were five that didn't. They got

72

hysterical, more or less—the mate was telling me—and they wouldn't leave the ship. And they said it was no trouble to get in the dory—they had lots of dories, no end of dories—and they went out. It wasn't rough at all. Only a heavy roll coming in. And when they left the ship it was in the nighttime—they could hear the other fellows hollering and hollering for them. And that's the last they ever heard of them. And when the boat hit—they said they hit west of where the boat came in, but they didn't. Because the *Marshall Frank* came in from the eastward and went up right on the gut rocks [in Marie Joseph Inlet]—put her bow right up on it. And she listed in. And if they had stayed on board they could have walked off without wetting their socks, low tide. But anyhow, those 5 finally left the boat. And that's all they heard of them after the hollering. But the reef the boat hit is the one east there—it's shoal, shoal water—from the end of the bank to the Big Breaker—it's a shoal, shoal reef—well, that's where they hit. I know that's where they hit.

See, when those five men left the boat there, they went for shore—well, it's only a couple of fathoms of water—there's always breakers any sea at all, at all. And they all got drowned. The five of them. (*So after the rest left the boat, those five decided to try to come in.*) Well, they must have. That's what the mate was telling me. "They started hollering and we didn't see them anymore. And the hollering stopped." But in the morning when I was talking to him, he said, "We're not sure what happened to them. I'm kind of afraid they got drowned, but I'm not too sure."

Okay. I got my cousin, you know, Donald John—and we took the horses, and we took them back down after they had breakfast at our place—and she was in full sail, boy, there on the rocks. And when we got down there, the big bank, there were three of the bodies ashore then. So we picked them up and we took them up to Uncle Kenny's barn. Took them in a sleigh then. And put them in there. Well, from there they took them to Sydney. I suppose the R.C.M.P. looked after them. But the other two, there were several days lapsed—maybe four or five days, anyhow—there wasn't a sign of the other two. And it's the funniest thing. This day, a dory landed at English Cove Pond—well, that's just about a half mile on the road—and wasn't one of them landed with the dory! He used to be in it, but it was upside down—when the dory landed he was there, too. He must have been in the dory and hanging on for life. And it's a funny thing we never saw that dory. I had a good pair of binoculars, and that high bank, and the day after she went there it was as smooth as glass. And looking, see if you could see anything—and we could never pick it up. And it landed. Well, so much for that fellow.

Now the last fellow, he landed in July. Where the first three landed. At Rock Hall, he landed there. And I know what happened, that kept him that long from landing. Just by this what we call the Rock Hall—it's shoal water all on the western side where the other fellows went. And there is a hole there maybe about four or five fathoms deep—maybe as long as from here to the road square. Quite deep. I used to put traps in there. And he must have got in the kelp in that, and that was in July sometime. I didn't see this fellow but they said—you know, he bloated when the weather got warm, and he floated and came in. But in that hole there's nothing but kelp, and I suppose he was tied down there, maybe a kind of a storm loosened [him]—but he came ashore in July.

And if they had stayed on board, there wasn't a drop of water in her. She just ran up there, boy—she had full sails on her. When they left the sails were on her. And of course the wind was from the southeast—not a storm by any means. She ran up as neat as anything. Her bow went up onto the rocks.

Where they abandoned the vessel, that's not where the boat was the next morning. They hit the reef between Framboise Cove—which would be about—what would it be, Malcolm? A third of a mile?

Malcolm MacDonald, Fourchu: Yes. It's also the possibility that she may have gone on the Big Breaker.

Dan Norman: Well no, Malcolm, she could never have gone on the Big Breaker. Well now, of course, you're never too sure what she did. But I figure that's the reef she went on, on account of where the men got drowned, see? They wouldn't have drowned leaving the ship at the Big Breaker.

Malcolm: No. What I mean by that, Dan Norman, was the first time she hit—she could have gone on the Big Breaker and come off it—and then the other people got off because there's deep water on the inside of the Big Breaker. You know, when they got out of her. And then she could have sailed on—then she'd go right possibly in the same direction. One of the reasons it's so hard to pinpoint is that we don't know where the last five got out.

Dan Norman: Well anyway, there was no trouble to get off on the outside—which there wouldn't, there wouldn't at all. And the only reason I think that's where she hit, because the way the wind was, it would take her dead on where she went. If it was the Big Breaker, Malcolm, she'd be liable to go west a long long ways before she hit. So you're never too sure, but that's my theory and I'm quite one hundred per cent sure—because three of them men were on the shore right opposite that reef. And the reef is—we'll say a quarter of a mile from the beach. Very shoal water from this reef. And they were landed the next day. Now if it was the Big Breaker, they certainly wouldn't have landed the next day. There's no way they'd have landed there. And she was heading west, you know. She was loaded with fish—all kinds of codfish in her.

When she hit, everybody abandoned the boat but those five—they wouldn't leave. The rest left. But after they left the boat, those fellows start hollering. They changed their mind. There must have been awful confusion in the first place, when they wouldn't go with the captain and the mate and the rest of them, you know. And the weather wasn't bad. And when they left [the last five men], I suppose they made for shore. Well, there's no damn way they'd get to shore, right there, in the dory. Too rough.

Malcolm: The ones that survived, they went out to sea. They didn't land. They went out in the dories and stayed out on the ocean till daylight.

Dan Norman: They went out to sea. The weather was all right. Nothing wrong with the weather, only there was a roll on—but they went out to sea and they waited for daylight. Why come ashore in the night? And the sea so smooth, no bad sea. Big double dories.

She was, I suppose, one of the last schooners—she was a genuine schooner, just like the *Bluenose*. On the same model exactly. She had been just refitted. She was on a maiden voyage after a refit. (*And they had been fishing.*) Oh, yeah. But I'm after forgetting where were they heading for—Lunenburg or somewheres. They were heading west, wherever they were heading. They were all Newfoundlanders. I heard from a fellow, Gerald Beaton from Sydney—he went on a cruise with this fellow that built a cement boat. It was years after the wreck—maybe it was five or six years ago. They went over to St. Pierre and they went to Newfoundland. And they went into this port, and there was a graveyard there. And Gerald was interested in that, see what kind of names were in it, you know. And here there's names for I don't know how many of the *Marshall Frank*—buried there. And on the tombstone there, where they got shipwrecked at Framboise, Cape Breton.

•

FROM A *CAPE BRETON POST* INTERVIEW, 1949: CAPTAIN ABE MILES of the *Marshall Frank*

I knew there was no hope for the ship and to tell the truth I felt there was no hope of getting ourselves to safety.

The boys didn't want to take to the dories. They said there wasn't a chance and they wanted to stay and die on the ship. I told them I was going over the side. I got into a dory with two crewmen. Then the crew decided to follow.

We were a quarter of a mile from shore. The coast is very rocky there. We abandoned ship in 10 minutes about 4 a.m. and there was no hope of getting in to the coast then. I had to lead the way and get soundings and then call the men to follow me. I left with two men in one dory. The deck was covered with ice making it very slippery. Water was pouring into the cabin when we went over the side. The bottom was torn out amidships.

The men lost were the last five on the ship—they refused to come off. They figured their chances were nil and they wanted to stay with her. Later we saw them getting into a dory and that was the last time we saw them.

We were all soaked and we rowed out to sea for 6 miles to wait for daybreak and try to get into land. It's ironic that we were only a quarter of a mile from land but had to turn for the open sea to survive. The five dories were in a line. We waited for the sixth dory but it never came.

We kept up the conversation as the five dories huddled together waiting for dawn. We never bothered with lifebelts. We were scared to move because of the big breakers. We were bouncing around in black fog like rubber balls.

When we got in, the first dory turned over and the men had to wade to shore. The other dories struck the shore side on and there was no difficulty reaching the beach.

DAN NORMAN MACLEOD: But it wasn't a storm that put them there at all. The weather was fair enough. (*So what put them there?*) Aw, they got off course. I think there were snow squalls. Nothing worse than snow on the water. I was coming down once—when I brought the boat down, coming across from Canso to Petit-de-Grat—and we struck a northwester there. You couldn't face it. And snow? Well, I never—I thought fog was bad enough, it's nothing compared with snow. It's absolutely the zero.

Malcolm MacDonald, Fourchu: Even radar doesn't work in the snow.

Dan Norman: And we had no radar anyhow. (*What did you do when you faced it?*) Well, we kept going. The fellow that was with me, an old fellow, he remembered from Yarmouth to Fourchu—he could name you every rock and island that was there. He was on the coasters years—what they called the coasters, you know. Years back, every port was supplied. Not the way it is [today]. There were no trucks in those day. And Fourchu and Gabarus and St. Peters and L'Ardoise and all—they used to call them coasters, small steamers. And he was on them for years. And every place you're coming along, he'd name every hole for you.

But we were coming across that day from Canso. It was blowing all right, but I went in to make something to eat. And he called to me after awhile. It was blowing. Snow?—aw, and blow—we're hitting the tide rips. The causeway wasn't there then. And you wouldn't believe it, she was going straight on end—a forty-footer. He wanted to go back to Canso. "Well," I said, "we're out halfways crossed to Cape Breton"—right in the tide rips, you know—ah, blowing. "Now," I said, "we'll keep her going. Do you know where Petit-de-Grat and Green Island are?" "No," he says, "I never...." "Well," I said, "we'll take a shot at it." You could pretty well tell by the map about where we should run. I said, "If you go back in this weather, man, you're going with the wind right on shore. If you go St. Peters Bay, well you're only getting the lee— what the heck, nothing can happen." We kept going. Well, it cleared off. Aw, we would have split Green Island!

The Loss of the *Marshall Frank*
by K. D. MacAskill, Point Michaud

Come listen to my story, pray lend to me an ear,
It's of those hardy men from Newfoundland with hearts that knew no fear.
They left their berth on the fishing banks, a westerly course to steer,
But came to grief on that treacherous reef their good ship did not clear.

All people that do live on shore, how will we ever know,
The dangers of the ocean while we are safe on shore.
While we did sleep in slumber deep, and for awhile our worries o'er,
Five brave lads were dying hard all off Framboise shore.

The *Marshall Frank* was as strong a ship as ever sailed the foam,
On that ill-fated night she left the banks with Halifax as her goal.
She was strongly built in Lunenburg of one hundred tons or more,
But her strength did fail when she came to bay
                        with the rocks off Framboise shore.

With her storm sail set and her foresail bent, this gallant ship glides on,
With the wind abeam and slightly careened while her engines hummed a song.
The weather thick with snow and sleet while frost did fill the air,
With an awful crash her timbers smashed and then her doom was there.

The captain gave orders to his crew to leave the ship at once,
With foaming breakers all around they thought their life was spent.
With seamanship they worked their way through and went to sea once more,
To God above they prayed for light so they could see the shore.

All through the night they were tossed about and circled 'round and 'round,
The dory they missed was number six, it was nowheres to be found.
With gloomy faces they knew their fate, they heard oh not a sound,
Down in their hearts they knew too well that five brave men were drowned.

Five brave men from Newfoundland, their toil on earth is o'er,
There is nothing left but broken hearts with loved ones that do mourn.
We hope that God has piloted them on, to a brighter and happier shore
Where no one weeps and loved ones meet, and never part no more.

And now to end my story, I'm bound to let you know
What did remain of five brave men where picked up on the shore.
They were taken back to their native land and loved ones that do mourn,
And given a decent burial in the land that they adore.

The Wreck of the *Hurry On* near Judique, Inverness County, 1935

On September 23, 1935, the motorship *Hurry On* went down about twenty miles off the Judique coast of Inverness County. The ship listed in the storm and the crew got to the only undamaged lifeboat. Waves overturned the boat, and some of the crew floated away and the oars were lost. Those left somehow righted the lifeboat, only to be swamped again. The survivors were eventually driven ashore at Judique, below the home of Dougald F. MacDonald—the lifeboat jammed between rocks. Otherwise, probably none of the crew would have had the strength to keep the boat beached.

What follows is a composite of news accounts, a few memories, and a wonderful poem composed by Euphemia Malcolm MacEachern. The poem was made shortly after the wreck, and became a song for a while in the community. As recently as a few years ago it was recited at the local school by Euphemia's granddaughter.

When the *Hurry On* Went Down
by Euphemia Malcolm MacEachern

High and dry on Judique Beach
In a cold and dreary dawn
'Twas a lifeboat with a crew of eight
From the steamer *Hurry On.*

A crew of eight? No, seven now
For just as they reached the shore
MacLean has closed his weary eyes
To open them nevermore.

Now five of them exhausted lay
They could not raise a hand

They did not know their little craft
Had washed up on the sand

But two there were could make their feet
They struggled bravely on
They climbed a bank and saw a house
And they knew the fight was won.

'Twas Dougald F. MacDonald's home
Close by the Judique shore
They stumbled weakly up to it
And knocked upon the door.

79

The good folk quickly took them in
And listened to their tale
Of how the good ship *Hurry On*
Had foundered in the gale.

How they had manned the
                    lifeboat then
And faced the raging storm
They hadn't time to salvage food
Nor clothes to keep them warm.

How these twelve men, so helpless
Upon the waves were tossed
Till breakers wild upset their craft
And four of them were lost.

They righted her and eight still lived
Tho' far from safe and sound
For hours and hours they tossed about
And then were washed aground.

"O haste, make haste, and help
                    these men
Or they will soon be dead"
The Judique men jumped to their feet
And to the shore they sped

They brought them in and carefully
They tended one and all
Tho' at the time they thought that two
Had heard the final call

But soon they rallied one by one
And to the Lord gave thanks
They said "He must have guided us
To land on Judique Banks"

For Judique hospitality
Is known throughout the land
'Tis part of their religion
To help their fellow-man.

And so these men from the *Hurry On*
Will long recall the names
Of Dougald F. MacDonald
And his brother, Willie James.

Now they're in St. Mary's Hospital
Reported doing fine
If you'd care to hear their names
We have them here in Rhyme.

There was Boudreau, Boyd and Baker,
And Carmichael as you know
One was Shode and one was Evans
And one Cocopardo.

So this concludes the story
Of the brave men who were saved
But God have mercy on those
                    poor souls
Who met a watery grave

And God have pity on those at home
And help them bear their cross
The mothers, wives, and fathers,
Who are left to mourn their loss

And O kind people safe on land
Won't you hearken to my plea
Say a prayer tonight and every night
For our boys who follow the sea.

from Newspaper Accounts and Memories

FIVE PERISH AS SHIP FOUNDERS
Are Washed From Mates' Tiring Arms
Seamen of *Hurry On* Deny Tossing Bodies From Lifeboat
Land At Judique

JUDIQUE, September 24, 1935—Five men died in the grip of giant combers and numbing cold, their bodies, all save one, washed ashore from the tiring arms of their almost unconscious mates as the crew of the Halifax motorship *Hurry On* were tossed in the pitiless Atlantic after their ship sank early Monday evening.

A water-filled lifeboat, freighted with one dead body and seven unconscious men, washed up on the shores of this little Cape Breton vil-

Wreck of the *Hurry On*, 1935

lage at dawn today, brought first news of the tragedy.

On his hands and knees one seaman dragged himself to a nearby house to seek aid. Villagers found in the boat the dead body of one of the crew, three unconscious men, and on the beach a fourth overcome by exposure and exhaustion.

PEGGY RANKIN, Frenchvale (daughter of Dougald F. MacDonald): My mother and father slept downstairs. And they just heard somebody doing this along the wall. (*Sort of scratching or rubbing?*) No, just trying to keep themselves standing, I guess. Just kind of rubbing along. So, my mother woke up right quick. And she said, "Dougald, there's somebody out there." So he jumped up. Just had to go around the corner and to the door. When he got to the door, those fellows came in. And they were frozen. There were two. Now I can't tell you what two they were. One of them was this Carmichael. Those two came in first. Then they described to my father what had happened and where the men were, which was below our farm like, on the shore. So, no phones or anything like that.

So my father got the boys out and sent one to my uncle's [James MacDonald] and one to Chisholms, which lived next on the other side—but they were farms, they were long runs. So he went down himself to the shore. At that time, there was one dead in the boat—you know, they just kept him in the boat till it landed. They got the other fellows up. But they had to make—it was down over a rocky—they had to carry them a little piece, you know.

So they landed them all back up at the house. And in the meantime, Mama had got the kitchen fire going and got the blankets lined up—so as soon as they'd come in they'd strip off as much as they could of their clothes and wrap them in wool blankets. And there was a good fire on, so they revived. And my father always had a little flask of brandy, because he had a heart condition and he found if he took a little brandy at that time, that it would help him. So they had a little brandy to cheer them up...

According to the story they had—from my father—was they left Halifax with a load of grain—corn, it was. And off the coast of our place there, a gale came up and the corn shifted. And the boat listed over and they thought she was going. And I guess the cap-

81

tain was trying to move the cargo back. Capt. Gardiner drowned. They found his body after I came home. They found it down quite a piece below our beach. It was a month later that they found his body.

(*What other story did people suggest made the* Hurry On *go down?*) This was the only story they had then. (Recently) somebody told me that it was owned in Halifax and that it was a rumrunner. Now that's utter hearsay. I don't know about that. But I can't see if it was, why the cargo would shift. The corn sounds more logical to me.

(*The news accounts of the day had a headline that said something like "Crew Denies They Threw People Overboard."*) Well, I remember my father saying that one of the men told him that they could have all got off quietly and into the lifeboats and did it—but that Capt. Gardiner wasn't allowing them to get off because he wanted to save the boat and he kept them on. And in the end of it, it was just jump in your [life]boat. Now one of the men told Dad that. And it sounds like they didn't come really prepared into the lifeboats. So that sounds like a right story....

They didn't have time to salvage food...and that sounds kind of right now, that [the captain] kept them busy. [The poem says] "they hadn't time to salvage food nor clothes to keep them warm." And that's what it looked like. My father said that. He said, "Gosh, for people jumping into a lifeboat, they should have taken heavy jackets and things"—they didn't. I guess mostly sweaters and things that they had on. I think [in the pictures] that's my father's sweaters. But he said they weren't clothed at all. The ones that died just really froze to death, with the wet and the cold.

Boat Twice Overturns

A furious storm that caused the *Hurry On* to founder after she had developed a 35-degree list beat about them all night.

Twice their lifeboat was overturned, twice they climbed back into a boat filled with chilling water and saw their mates die one by one. Somewhere off the rocky Cape Breton coast four bodies drift tonight.

The *Hurry On* was bound from Halifax to Montreal with a cargo of corn and cleared from Halifax Sunday morning.

Twenty-three miles off this port, as she emerged from the Strait of

Wreck of the *Hurry On*, 1935

Canso into the lower Gulf of St. Lawrence, she was caught in a roaring gale, made worse by the shallow waters off that section of the coast. As she pitched and rolled in great seas, every available sailor of her crew of 12 was put to work pouring oil on the waters but to no avail.

Washed From Tiring Arms Of Their Mates

Battered far over to starboard until the tip of her funnel almost touched the wild seas, the one lifeboat left that could be launched was equipped and lowered. For ten minutes they stood by and then the *Hurry On* sank at seven o'clock.

Twenty-five minutes later a huge comber rolled over the boat as they battled to reach shore and safety—and overturned it. When they climbed back, provisions and oars were gone. Again the battering waves overturned their craft and while they were righting it Mate Alexander MacKenzie, North Sydney, cried: "I'm all in," and sank directly.

Huddled on the bare seats with chilling water swirling around them, rain and hail beating into their faces and the boat lurching drunkenly beneath them as wave after wave beat against it, they sat and waited for death....

Eighteen-year-old donkeyman Alex Wait of Sceptre, Sask., died from injuries and exposure a few hours later. He went without a word, the survivors said.

Captain Gardner was the next to go. Weakened by cold and exposure, he whispered a "Pray for me, boys," lost his hold on the seat as his crew watched powerless to aid, and slipped overboard as the seas plucked at his body. It was about two hours after.

Then the paralyzing cold gripped the mate, J.F. MacAulay of North Sydney, a cousin of Dr. MacAulay, North Sydney, and he too lost his grip and went overboard.

Only an hour away from land and life, Fraser MacLean of Pictou Island succumbed. His was the body found in the boat after it beached. It was lodged under a thwart.

Couldn't Hold Bodies

"We tried to stow all of them under the thwarts but there was no rope to tie them with," Albert Boudreau, native of Arichat, told. "The first thing we would know a man would disappear and we were in no shape to hold them in the boat."

At dawn after a night of horror and death, a chance wind blew the craft ashore. With Chief Engineer Schade, Gus Carmichael crawled to the home of William [Dougald] J. MacDonald at South Judique, begging for help and muttering deliriously.

When hastily summoned residents arrived at the shore, they found Lawrence Cacopardo clinging to the dead body of Fraser MacLean. On their way they had found the unconscious form of Albert Boudreau, lying in a field where he had crawled. He was unconscious until noon.

Not Thrown Out

A coroner's inquest held over the body of Fraser MacLean, whose dead body was found in the boat, held there by a thwart, decided death was caused by exposure. Two of the witnesses, Boudreau and Fraser, were alleged to have told the coroner's jury the bodies of the other victims were thrown out to lighten the boat, but both later denied it was so. "We were only half-conscious then," they said. "We might have said anything."

Stops Engines

"Between seven and 14 miles off Henry Island, the *Hurry On* listed to starboard," Chief Engineer Schade, native of Hamburg but now a naturalized Canadian, said. "We set all pumps in operation and the engines were ordered stopped. It was about 5:30.

"The pumps proved unavailing and at 6:45 the lifeboat was lowered. There was a list of about 35 degrees then. The boat on the bridge was battered to pieces by the giant seas and the port boat couldn't be launched on account of the list.

"Ten minutes later the *Hurry On* sank and about 15 minutes later the [life]boat capsized. The men managed to right her, but everything in it had been swept away. When it overturned the second time, First Mate MacKenzie said, 'Boys, [I'm] all in,' and sank. The rest of the [men] crawled back in. Then Capt. Gardiner and Alex Wait died in the boat. Third Engineer MacAulay was overcome by cramps and fell over. The rest of us were exhausted."

Mountainous Seas

"Four mountainous seas landed the lifeboat on shore between...large rocks and the six of us crawled ashore. The Cook Lawrence Cacopardo we thought was dead. Gus Carmichael and myself were the only ones able to crawl, and we set off for help." They reached Dougald

Wreck of the *Hurry On*, 1935

MacDonald's home at about 5:45, and [wakened] the household. The rescue party, consisting of Dougald MacDonald, his son William, Dan Chisholm, John MacDougall, and...girls, Mary E. Chisholm and Jeanette Fortune, left immediately in a truck.

Nurses and doctors were summoned, Drs. A.N. Chisholm and J.R. McLeod leaving immediately from Port Hawkesbury with R.C.M.P. Officer William MacDonald, and Mrs. Duncan MacLellan, R.N., leaving from Judique.

Off Port Hood

The *Hurry On* foundered about 6:30 Monday night 10 miles off Port Hood in a north-west gale, Albert Boudreau said. "Gus Carmichael's head was cut when the boat was being lowered," he told, and described the capsizing of the craft later.

"This is my second shipwreck," Lawrence Cacopardo, native of Malta but for some years residing at 173 Maynard Street, Halifax, said. "I was chief cook and steward on the salvage tug *Reindeer* when she foundered off Sable Island. We left Canso about 8 a.m. Monday. The wind began to increase until about ten miles off Port Hood it was blowing a hurricane with rain and hail. The cargo of corn which we carried shifted, and we took to the boats. The ship sank at 6:30 and my watch stopped at 6:33," he said.

The second time the boat overturned, Albert Boudreau dived under the boat and retrieved the almost unconscious body of Lawrence Cacopardo, but Mate MacKenzie sank so quickly, no one was able to aid him, the youthful engineer said. Before Fraser MacLean died, the survivors said, they had wanted to help him, but he waved them back and said, "Take care of yourselves."

·   ·   ·

A Mounted Police plane was despatched here from Sydney early today, and a vessel came down from Port Hawkesbury, and aiding in the search for a time were three planes from the Cape Breton Flying Club led by Lindsay Rood, pilot instructor.

Meanwhile, in St. Mary's Hospital, Inverness, the seven survivors are gradually recovering from the harrowing experience Monday, hospital officials stated tonight. H.H. Herman, Chief Engineer, who attendants feared was threatened with pneumonia yesterday, came around satisfactorally today and is in no danger.

85

REMAINS OF THE CAPTAIN AND THIRD ENGINEER ARE FOUND

Farmer Taking Cows To Pasture Makes Discovery— Identification Is Easily Made

JUDIQUE, October 6, 1935—The sea has given up two of the *Hurry On* victims as early on Sunday Morning the bodies of Capt. A.H. Gardiner and James F. MacAulay, third engineer of the ill-fated freighter, were found washed up on the Judique shore. Torn and worried by sea currents since the stormy night of Sept. 23, when their exhausted hands could no longer cling to the tossed life boat, the bodies show comparatively little decomposition for the period of time they have been in the water, said Dr. J.R. MacLeod of Port Hawkesbury, coroner, who examined the bodies. There will be no inquest, he further stated.

Watch will be kept for the bodies of the other two victims, as yet unaccounted for, Mate Alex MacKenzie and the eighteen year old donkeyman, Alex Wait. In the meantine the body of Capt. Gardiner is on its way to Halifax in Zinck's ambulance, while that of James MacAulay has been forwarded to Orangedale for interment.

Taking his cows to pasture about seven o'clock this morning Allan MacDonald noticed an object lying on the shore and on going down to investigate found the remains of a man. Tattoo marks on an arm identified him as Captain Gardiner.

Nearby residents were notified and after the body was removed to a farm building, search was proceeded with along the shore, and about 100 yards from the dory which the castaways of the *Hurry On* had succeeded in making their escape in, was found the body of Third Engineer MacAulay.

AGNES POUSHAY, Sydney: The boy that was drowned that we knew [James F. MacAulay], he lived [at River Denys] about eighteen miles from our home [at Marble Mountain]. And we knew them well, we knew the family well. He was a third-year engineering student. And as I understood, he was to have some practical experience to get his degree. And the man who owned the boat would be a relative by marriage of MacAulay. I'm not sure what the connection was....

(*One person thought he was a boyfriend of yours.*) No, no. I knew him well and we did correspond. I think he did probably have a girlfriend. It's just that we were friends and he did write me just before he went on this trip. He did say, "I'll bring you back a souvenir from Holland." But there had been a change in plans....

And the Wait boy who was also buried [here]—I think, I'm not sure, they removed the remains some years later—he was buried at the request of the MacAulays, that he was buried right beside his friend. He was only a young fellow, eighteen—and I don't know if it says in that article but I remember them saying at the time that he had died in the MacAulay boy's arms. See, they died on the way to shore. They died just as they got to shore or on the way to shore.

They got the MacAulay boy first. And I'm quite sure that while we were there [at the wake] a phone call came saying that the Wait boy's body had been found—and I think he was buried the next day. I don't remember if the service for Wait was in the house but I remember well being at the cemetery when he was being interred. MacAulays looked after that. I don't know why. But anyway it's a long way to the West Coast [the Wait boy's home] and at eighteen, if you're down here—I'm sure there was some reason for it. I'm sure [family] took his remains back later on. I know they did visit the cemetery later on.

It was a fairly largely attended funeral. Most of the friends of MacAulays were there. But I don't believe there was even one person there who had ever seen the [Wait] boy. But I remember a call coming from Halifax while we were there, I believe from a girlfriend—I don't know the name. I'm quite sure we were waiting for the remains to come from Judique to the MacAulay residence—while we were there—that this girl called, to say her thoughts were there. I suppose she was only a young girl. He was eighteen....

FRIEND VOLUNTEERS EULOGY OF ALEX MACKENZIE

One who knew him, writes of Alex MacKenzie: "May I be allowed to say a word about one whom many seafaring men in Nova Scotia will remember as a true and faithful comrade—I refer to Alex MacKenzie, whose name is listed among the lost in the dreadful disaster to the *Hurry On*. Alex was a thoroughly good fellow, in spite of a rough manner one of Nature's gentlemen, and one of the most generous-hearted men

I ever knew. He was a native of Cape Breton Island, North Sydney, I believe, and had followed the sea from his youth, and in his thirty-odd years as a sailor he had been several times round the world, had sailed every sea, and had helped to steer his ship safely in and out of almost every sea-port in every country of the world. It is a strange fate which decreed that his last sight of land should be the shores of his native isle."

PEGGY RANKIN: (*I don't suppose any of the people who took in the survivors are living today. Your father....*) No. James, nor Annie nor Sadie, James's wife—there's none of those people still living. And James' wife just died here two years ago. Some of them went down to her place. I know they were telling a story that one of them had died and they had just put the remains in the milk house. [After that], every time we would go to the milk house for Sadie, we used to be looking sideways. Laughing. When you're kids, you know, you think it's—oooo.

(*Doesn't your husband Donald tell a story about a fiddler?*) I think they were having a few that night. That's why everybody was on deck down at James' place.... I think it was Duncan that was telling Donald the stories. I think they were just fooling around with [the fiddler, Robert]. He was only a little, little man. And my uncle was quite a big rugged man. And one of those fellows that drowned, that they found the body, was kind of a heavy-set fellow. So I guess Robert [the fiddler] had a little snooze. And then he came out. And this Duncan told him, "You and James had kind of a tiff last night." "Oh, did we? did we?" he said. And Duncan said, "I guess you did. Come here." Showed him this in the outhouse. Robert nearly died. He didn't really look at him. He looked at a big fellow and he thought, "What did I do with him?" "Fought with him. And killed him." Oh, my. Duncan had to catch him. He was going down in a pile.

Fishermen Rescue American Seamen at Louisbourg, 1943

by Jean Kyte, including conversations with Charlie Bagnell and Ed Levy

Oddly enough, there were two separate rescues of American seamen at the mouth of Louisbourg Harbour, 1943. Two groups went out apparently unknown to one another, and each group rescued some of the seamen trapped aboard the *Sub-Chaser 709*—and at least to Walter Boudreau (as we'll learn in the next chapter), it was many years before he knew of the two events. Had he stayed longer in Louisbourg, he would have learned. But after he participated in the rescue he sailed away on the *Angelus*—sailing into what became another ship's sinking. Captain Boudreau's story begins on page 95. But we begin with the *S.C. 709*, stranded and caked in ice on a bar in the mouth of Louisbourg Harbour with twenty-fix seamen on board, freezing to death. Along with *Cape Breton's Magazine* interviews with fishermen Charlie Bagnell and Ed Levy, here is Jean Kyte's telling of one of the heroic rescues.

THE *S.C. 709* was commissioned at Elizabeth City, North Carolina, in November 1942. Her captain was Lieut. William C. French, Jr., and her ensign Albert D. Jordan, and she had a crew of twenty-four. She was 120 feet long with a beam of twenty feet, and carried one three-inch and two twenty-millimetre guns, along with twenty depth charges. She also carried sound gear, radar and submarine detection equipment.

She operated out of Portland, Maine, during the fall and early winter, and on January 16, 1943, was ordered to Argentia, Newfoundland. She got under way on January 18 in company with the *U.S.C.G. Storis* under a grey sky. On the morning of the 19th the rain and mist commenced. About 1415 (2:15 p.m.) the rain became continuous. At 1756 the commanding officer advised the *Storis*, "Our radar out of commission, will do our best to keep up to you during the night." This was the last time contact was made with the *Storis*.

On January 20 ice was beginning to form and occasional chipping was required. At 1351 land was sighted off the port bow and identified as Egg Island. Ice continued to form and was chipped off and it was felt to be under control. A return to Halifax would have necessitated running into the sea and entering at night, so it was decided to continue up the coast.

The official U.S. Navy report records the grim battle with the Atlantic: "Prior to midnight ice commenced to form with such speed that all hands (available) were ordered to chip ice. The ice was of a soft nature making chipping with any haste impossible.... The deck, particularly along the port side, was covered with about a foot of ice...the bridge ports save two being completely covered with ice.... The crew was becoming physically exhausted and the temperature was well below zero. Before an area could be cleared enough to see anything of the ship proper, the previously chipped area would be filled in again. Chipping teams were established, two men working from five to ten minutes. Sleep was impossible."

During the night the storm increased and the ice grip on the ship tightened. Between 0321 and 0410 the engineer officer and gunner's mate succeeded in clearing the depth charge projectors and fired them. At 0504 George Gagnon was washed overboard into the icy water but was rescued. The ship was now listing to port twenty-five degrees. Ammunition was moved to starboard and amidships, but the ship still listed five to ten degrees. The ice buildup continued and from Egg Island on, navigation was by dead reckoning.

At 0755 course was changed for Louisbourg. "Ice continued to form, in fact it was impossible to chip successfully. All hands were wet through and physically exhausted." Visibility at sunrise was estimated at 500 yards, the sea at force eight and the wind about fifty miles an hour. At 0900 the ice was beyond control, and by this time the decision was made to beach the ship. At 1100 general visibility had closed to 300 yards, but at 1122 through a brief lift in the storm, a single church was observed. (It was St. Bartholomew's Anglican Church, a Louisbourg landmark since 1885.) A few minutes later another quick view was had of several freighters and some rocks in what appeared to be a harbour. At 1126 the ship took a fifty-degree list to port due to heavy ice formation and to the fact that the sea that had previously held the vessel on a reasonably even keel had subsided, the vessel now being protected by the beach. The captain tried several courses to clear the rocks, but the ship, now a floating iceberg (she was covered from bow to stern with about fifty-five tons of ice, according to Yeoman Peter Federspiel in later testimony), would not respond to any rudder. At 1131 the *S.C. 709* struck the reef in the harbour approach to Louisbourg. All hands were ordered to topside with life jackets.

Visibility was still very poor, but the Pilot Station at Louisbourg had noted the ice-coated vessel and alerted the Canadian Navy. Hyacinth Pottie, coxswain of the Navy harbour craft, was among the personnel who attempted to reach the ship. "We could see them clinging to the deck," he recalled, "but we couldn't reach them with the high seas. We couldn't even get a line on her." The U.S. Navy report: "During this time the majority of the crew were huddled in the pilot house (of the ship).... During the later part of the afternoon, the Commanding Officer ordered all hands out of the pilot house because it appeared that the vessel might capsize to port.... Many line rockets were fired but never once did they get close enough." Prior to this time all available gear for protection had been brought up from below. One of the ships in the harbour tried to float out a life raft, and the crew of the *Lady Laurier* shot line after line out to the men, in vain. The minimum recorded temperature during the twenty-four hours was two degrees Fahrenheit, and the maximum was nine degrees Fahrenheit.

CHARLIE BAGNELL, Louisbourg: They were up on deck all night. And they went there about ten o'clock in the morning. It was a bitter, bitter cold night. The Navy had charge of everything here then. Those men had been out there all night, all day till ten o'clock in the morning. With the vapour flying, sometimes you could see the ship and sometimes you couldn't. Earl Lewis, he was with the Fishery Department at that time—he had called Ottawa and reported it, because it was in his jurisdiction, too. Ottawa told him that the Navy said, "The salvage operations were progressing favourably." And there was nobody off then. Those men were freezing to death. Something had to be done.

THE THREE-MASTED Norwegian barquentine *Angelus*, Captain Jensen, was in port. Four crewmen, Walter Boudreau, Moncton New Brunswick, Clarence Mullins and John Hillier, Belleoram, Newfoundland, and Joseph Chiasson, New Waterford, Nova Scotia [later, we learned that he was Yvon Joseph Chiasson of Belle Cote, Inverness County, Cape Breton], took two dories up to Burying Ground Point [now part of the National Park], and launched them. Contending with the wind and sea, they managed to row to the stricken ship.

At the same time, L.H. Cann, owner-manager of a ship repair shop on the harbour front, and Earl Lewis, Fisheries Inspector, met with Louisbourg fishermen, and a rescue attempt by them was decided upon.

The rescue crew from Louisbourg was made up of the Bagnell brothers, Charlie, Nelson and Joe, Wilbert Goyetche, Ed Levy and Earl Lewis. They used Goyetche's boat, the *W.G.*, which had a shallow draft, sometimes used as a pilot boat and mainly to deliver stores to ships for Lewis & Company.

CHARLIE BAGNELL: There was quite a lot of ice in the harbour at the time. When we were going down, we met one of the pilots—"Oh, damn it," he said, "you can't get near that, the ocean's a sea out there, you can't get near it." We went down anyway, to have a look. Had to wait for a tugboat to bring a boat down from the old town, that was up in the upper harbour. When he brought her down and docked her, then he made a road for us out, broke through the ice for us.

[Captain Jack Savory of the Dominion Coal Company tug, *Ascupart*, towed the *W.G.* as close as possible to the *S.C. 709* through the ice.]

ED LEVY, Louisbourg: "Because we couldn't pound our way to it—we'd smash the boat to pieces." (*The ice was solid?*) "No, no, it was kind of drift ice, it was cakes of ice. But it had been driven down here in the bottom of the harbour. Where the wind was southeast the night before, now the wind was off nor'west. But we didn't have to go very far—out, oh, perhaps a quarter of a mile through the ice. No more. And we got clear water. She was wide and our boat was only narrow and we went in behind her, kept right up tight to the stern. And we went out, over the bar, where they said no boat could go. Well, cripes, I'd go and Joe Bagnell'd go, Nelson used to go out through there every day when we were lobster fishing. It's not a very wide space. **Charlie:** Used to call it "the tail end of the bar." **Ed:** Yeah, it was as wide, I suppose, as the boat shop is long. (*Fifty feet.*) Yeah. Of course, she only drew two feet of water. **Charlie:** Not any more. **Ed:** 'Cause she was built with a shoal draft. And she went out over.

Charlie Bagnell: So we got out and got over the bar, and it was just a mass of white foam. First time we went over, we rounded up, we couldn't make it, we had to make a second circle. The crew were all standing on the deck, and were they ever cold—they couldn't straighten out their hands. We threw a line up, and I don't know how they got it around, but they got it around and jammed.

Ed Levy: Charlie's brother Joe was on the bow of her and he threw a rope up a couple times and they couldn't—the men were too frozen that they couldn't move—by and by he got a gaff and he gaffed it. The rope went in over her rail, her wire rail. Joe gaffed it back and held it, held the end of it. (*So they didn't take the rope from you.*) They couldn't. They were too cold. Man, you take—they were on deck of that thing from eleven o'clock in the morning one day and this was about eleven o'clock in the next day—twenty-four hours and with below zero weather, I'm telling you. And nothing to cover themselves with. Some with their bare feet, some with shoes on—almost all had bare hands. Some had socks on their feet. Oh man, dear, if you'd seen the mess those men were in.

When they rolled over the side of the boat and came down into the boat—and Joe and Nelson and Earl Lewis and you, Charlie, were at it too—and they'd take them over the side—the boat was up quite high—they'd let themselves go. You'd grab them and pull them in the boat. Their hands were frozen. The good ones helped the bad ones, see. The worst ones we took down forward. And the ones that could stand up—there were a couple of them— we left them stand up back in the back part of the boat.

I couldn't believe we were twenty-five to thirty minutes. **Charlie:** No more. **Ed:** From the time we left the tug [till] we were back to the tug. The tug was waiting for us on the end of the bar to bring us in through the ice. And I don't think we were an hour from the time we left the wharf till we were back to the wharf again.

Charlie Bagnell: It was eighteen we took off. Some of them had frostbite. I did hear a fellow lost a toe, I don't know whether that's right or not. Took them up to the Navy League. Oh, a very uncomfortable night. She pounded to pieces out there.

ALL WERE LANDED at Lewis's wharf, some so frozen they couldn't walk. All the men were immediately taken to the Navy League Hut (hostel) where townswomen, alerted, had set up an emergency hospital ward. Under Mrs. Catherine Lewis, R.N., and Mrs. Weir Martell, R.N., a team comprised of Mrs. Miriam Cameron, Mrs. Norma Covey, Mrs. Annie Dickson, Mrs. Sadie Dowling, Mrs. Retha Jewell, Mrs. Winnie Kyte, Mrs. Eva Lewis, Mrs. Bessie Mounce, Mrs. Alberta Stevens, R.N., Mrs. Ruby Stewart, Mrs. "Jimmy Ned" Townsend, and Mrs. Laura Wilcox, R.N., gently removed the iced clothes, bathed the men in warm water, patted circulation back into frozen limbs, wrapped the men in blankets and fed them soup and coffee, "the first hot food and coffee since our departure the previous Monday," commented Ensign Jordan. "Excellent and efficient care was taken of us, although we were too spent to care much." Other women in town made gallons of hot soup and coffee and sons and daughters were pressed into service to bring them up to the Navy Hut for the men.

It took an hour per man to revive them. As they revived they were taken to the Air Force Hospital in Victoria Park, Sydney. Not a man lost his life.

D.H. Gibson, C.B.E., then president of the Navy League, paid tribute to the men and women in a full-page ad in the August 23,

1943, *Montreal Gazette*, sponsored by the Robert Simpson Company for the 1943 Navy League appeal. Below a graphic drawing of the ice-caked ship and the small boat heading towards the anxious seamen, the caption read:

BY THEIR DEEDS, MEASURE YOURS

...These...men were exposed on the upper deck during the howling gale and fierce blasts of the winter wind and icy spray coating their clothing. They dare not go below for fear of their ship keeling over with the weight of ice. Rescued by gallant Louisbourg fishermen, they were brought into the Navy League Hostel.... Because of the care received at the hostel the limbs of all but one were saved.

Walter Boudreau:

The Louisbourg Rescue,

and the Sinking of the

Schooner *Angelus*, 1943

Walter Boudreau of the crew of the *Angelus* was among the men who rescued American sailors from the *S.C. 709* . He joined the *Angelus* in Louisbourg, participated in the rescue, finished loading and repairing the *Angelus*—and sailed from Louisbourg for Barbados. On their way back, the *Angelus* was stopped by a German submarine. The rescuers soon became shipwreck victims. But we'll let Walter Boudreau, one of the two survivors, tell his story. Ronald Caplan talked with him for *Cape Breton's Magazine*.

Part 1:
Rescue of the American Sailors

I WAS IN the Merchant Marine. And being in the Merchant Marine meant that we got jobs on ships of many nationalities going to different parts of the world. North Atlantic convoys, southern-bound convoys, and so on. So it just so happened that I had always wanted to sail on the square-rigger. I had just come off a Norwegian ship in the North Atlantic convoy system and I heard about this job in Halifax with the Shaw Steamship Company. And they said, "There's a square-rigger [the *Angelus*] up in Louisbourg loading for the West Indies." So I applied for the job and they sent me up there. I believe it was in January. And we were [in Louisbourg] through January into February loading lumber to take down to Barbados.

And then one day [while loading the *Angelus*] Captain Jensen said, "There's a wreck outside. A United States ship, naval ship, is wrecked on the reef." We didn't comment much on that, just ate our potatoes—which is about all we had. And then the following day he said, "They can't get the men off!" And it went on from there. I believe that Captain Jensen had been contacted, or contacted somebody in Louisbourg and said that he had, probably, some men who could—they had an idea how to reach that wreck. The idea was based on the fact that he was going to have us go around to a far point. I think there's a park there, or used to be; they called it Cemetery Point or something, way out far from Louisbourg town. [This is Burying Ground Point, now part of the Fortress of Louisbourg National Historic Park.] And so some people of Louisbourg provided us with a truck to give us a drive out there, and some new oars, and two dories which were upside down in the snow. And cut down the barbed wire fence. The only thing they didn't do was to get in the dories and row out to the wreck.

Now, meanwhile, the Louisbourg fishermen [who also res-

The Sinking of the *Angelus*, 1943

cued U.S. seamen] were in a completely different area—
somewhere down where the town wharf is. So we didn't know
anything about them, and they didn't know anything about us. We
left from a different place. We got there first, took the first eight
people off. And then we....

*(Don't be afraid to give me the details. What was the situation
when you got to Cemetery Point? Were you able to see the vessel
in trouble?)*

Are you a seaman? *(No, I'm not.)* If you give me a little paper,
I'll show you a lot better.... This is roughly the situation.... [Here,
Walter drew us a rough map.]

Here's Louisbourg Harbour, and that would be the town docks
and areas there. Then there's a point way out here, way out in the
country. Now then, there's a big reef goes out here, and the wreck
was on the outer Atlantic side of the reef. Now because of the ice
and everything, and the *Angelus* was out here somewhere on one
of these [town] docks—our captain decided: Well, we can't possibly get dories out through there because it's got too much ice.
(Louisbourg Harbour was iced over.) Well, partly, not solid. And
then there was this swell coming in [over the reef]. And the swell
was breaking, coming around and breaking. And then it was coming in here in waves that were fairly sizeable but not storm waves,
and then they'd curl. If you ever got into one of them or got under
one of them and they'd curl in and you get in that water—you're
dead, you know. How long do you live in that water? Three
minutes.

Anyway, Captain Jensen's idea was that we would get these
two dories which they located, and try and reach the wreck from
here. Shorter, avoiding all this ice. Now the Louisbourg fishermen, after we had done the original [run]—we were the one who
reached the boat. The Canadian Navy couldn't do it because of the
[shallow] water there and they just couldn't do it. I was one of the
two men in the first dory. In fact, I was the first man to get on that
ship. The reason I'm absolutely clear about that is that when we
got on the lee side of the boat, I took the oar and I hit the side—it
was just one block of ice—and then we could hear talk and voices
inside. And then they started to holler. We knocked down the
ice—you could see through a glass—and then they opened the

door and we got two men off. It was an Engineer Chief, I think, and somebody else. There were two men we took ashore, first trip. And then we went back a second trip.

Now, having done that, we had no knowledge of what was going on with the Louisbourg fishermen.

(*Okay, but take me back for a second. You've trucked your dories to Cemetery Point and—were both of your dories used in the first attempt? Did you both row out?*) Yes. One dory was behind the other because, I mean, we were told to get out there fast. The tide had something to do with it—but we were only the guys who were doing the rowing. But, in other words: Get out there while the going's good. And as I recall that was somewhere around 11:30 a.m.

(*How good was the going?*) It wasn't all that bad, but if you ever got caught in one of those [waves]—it was one of these deals where you'd have a sea breaking here, and one breaking there, and if you happened to get under it, well, that was it. But we had a dory that we could dance around and avoid them, you see. In other words, we might row this way and one of us would look and say, "There's one there." We'd go hard right. (*And you had that much control?*) Oh, a dory is very maneuverable; it's like a bicycle—if you know how to row it. And I mean, these are Newfoundlanders, and I'm an experienced boatman, so we knew how to handle it.

(*I see. How many of you were there in that dory?*) Two in each dory. (*How long did it take you to go from Cemetery Point out to the wreck of the S.C. 709?*) I seem to think it was around between twenty and thirty minutes. Something like that, maybe a little longer. (*Was there any doubt that you could get to the vessel?*) Well, yeah. We weren't sure we could get to the vessel. We were not sure. But we thought we could.

(*Now when you got to the Navy vessel, did you go aboard to get these men off?*) She was leaning over and we didn't go to the high side, we went to the sheltered side. And I was in the first dory. And I took my oar and pounded, got voices. There was one guy with a South Carolina accent who appeared at the window and he said, "Ooh, man. Is I ever glad to see you!" So we took off the first two men. And while we're going, the second dory is a hundred feet behind us. So that's why the two dories got out there—one first, and then another one a few minutes later.

The Sinking of the *Angelus*, 1943

So we took two and then they got in behind us and took two. We went in and we both went back on the second [trip]. Taking eight men. (*I see. And all these men were able to get off themselves?*) Well, they were in various stages. We were not in a position to fool around. I mean, when they came out we just grabbed them and sling them into the boat and get the hell out of there before we all get drowned, you know. It wasn't a case of, "Did you give them first aid?" And I said, "No, you just get them the hell on the boat and get ashore before we're all in the water!" And the fishermen mentioned that when they got there all the men were walking around the boat. Which proves again that they were there later than we were because when we got to the boat there was a block of ice and nobody could.... Nobody had been into that boat. And nobody had come out until we pounded. But once they started saying, "Well, there's rescue boats," naturally they all came out and scampered around the boat.

(*So, you brought them back to shore, and then what happened? Why did you not continue going out and bringing more people off?*) Well, I think, this second boat, I believe when they came back the fishermen had got there just as they were leaving, and I don't think there was anything for them to go back for. I think there was a motor boat was there, capable of taking larger groups. So they said, "Well, so we've got eight off and the other boat is taking the rest." And we were not too anxious to row out there again because my arms were just breaking, then, by this time, you know. It was hard rowing.

(*So where did you go from there?*) We took them to the same place [where the dories had been launched]. Right here on the edge just by this big, snowy field. And we had to knock down somebody's barbed wire fence. There was a road out there. So when we reached the beach there was somebody there that took them over and we don't know what happened to them because we turned around instantly and went back out.

(*After your second trip out and back, did you come into town with them?*) No. We didn't see anything of them at all. (*You didn't go to the party or the gathering?*) Other than the gathering, it seems to me it was in the evening from what I recall. We went back to our boat and I guess Captain Jensen was pleased with us, and we were pretty proud of ourselves—pretty happy that we saved the men. And that evening, I think it was, we went [to] one of those military places or some kind of a building. We were not taken there in a truck or given any transportation. We walked out...in the snow. And when we got there the Royal Canadian Navy was standing around; you know, tipping glasses. And we stood in the corner with our fur hats and ear muffs and mittens and rubber boots like dodos, and nobody paid any attention to us at all. I think somebody later came and gave us a drink, I seem to recall—or maybe it was coffee. And we said, "Well, we may as well go home." Which is what we did.

Now that was the last of the rescue as far as I was concerned. I never saw anything in print. A few days after that we were on our way....

(*And you never actually saw the Louisbourg fishermen.*) Never—never saw them. (*So perhaps they never saw you either, and these are two separate rescues. Do you think that's the case?*) Exactly. I think that's the case. And I don't think there's any deliberate effort by the fishermen to belittle us or push us out of this and get any credit that might be coming. I think they simply didn't know much about what took place way out here [at Cemetery Point]. Just as we knew nothing.... It was two distant points far apart. We didn't see each other.

(*Isn't that extraordinary? So two separate rescues were made and both cases, I think, still sound like two courageous rescues. Do you think it was? Courageous rescues?*) Yes, I do. Because we could have lost our lives. I mean if that's what you call "courage." Or, in my case, I just loved adventures. I've been in so many damn things—wrecks and experiences—and I loved it all. So, I mean, maybe half the time I was moved just because I like to be involved in situations.

(*And a couple of days later, you had your load of lumber in the hold of the* Angelus, *plus a deck load of lumber?*) Big deck load. Eleven feet high strapped onto the deck—lumber. (*And let me understand, the* Angelus *was not a steamboat.*) She's a square-rigger. The French fleet had been coming to North Sydney for years with these big four-masters on the way to the fisheries up in the Grand Banks and Iceland and Greenland. And they would, for many years, come in to North Sydney. And these were big square-rig sailing vessels. There's no more of them in the world left today....

Part 2:
Sinking the *Angelus*

A NYWAY, the story about the *Angelus* was that these vessels which had been sent up north, they were Portuguese owned, would load up [with] salt fish. They'd be away for, sometimes, almost a year. It's a very tough life for those guys. And they had the little dories. They were what they called eighty-man, eighty-dory schooners—eighty. Which is, you know, the Lunenburg fishermen like the *Bluenose* only carried maybe, I don't know, fifteen dories or maybe something like that. These were big vessels—eighty dories. And it was a tough life, very little pay, they were out a year, and then they'd go back.

So when the war came on, the Canadian government seized some of these ships which had been over here. And then a group in Halifax decided to run her on the West Indian trips. But, of course, those ships had to go without convoy. All the steamships were in convoy but when you signed on the *Angelus*, there's no convoy. You sail alone.

When you were out on one of those old square-riggers you were on your own, but there was one thing that—it was mistaken—but we thought, Well, we're safer because they're not going to bother us. Even if the subs see us they're not going to bother with us. Too small.

But it didn't work out that way because the subs sank many sailing vessels all through the West Indies....

(*Do you remember the day you sailed aboard the* Angelus *from Louisbourg?*) March. We were towed out of Louisbourg in ice, in quite heavy ice. This is one of the bad times of year in the North Atlantic. (*Where did they drop you?*) Maybe four or five miles outside. The old *Angelus* was not in very good shape. By this time she was leaking, I mean right away, as soon as we were outside the harbour, she was leaking. And they come and say, "Well, get

101

to the pumps." We never stopped pumping until they got to Barbados—and we had a very small crew. Watches were four hours on and four hours off. Normal sailing today is four on and eight off. So you have three watches. But this was an economy ship—two watches. Four hours on, four hours off. And oftentimes you'd stand your watch when you had been doing a lot of pumping, and then you'd crawl in bed with your rubber boots and everything else on, and try and get some sleep—and either one of the sails would blow out and you'd have to go up in the [yard]arms in the sleet and the cold, or get to the pumps during the time you're supposed to be in bed sleeping.

And this kept on being pretty rough going and pretty lousy until we finally got into it across the Gulf Stream. Still bumpy, but warm weather. And then we all started to get our health back and life was good. Captain Jensen was a very nice man. He was a little guy. But he was a good man....

And, all right, we got to Barbados and our boat didn't have any machinery—no engine. The only machinery was the alarm clock. No refrigeration. Nothing like fresh eggs or fruit or anything like that. Just potatoes, potatoes, salt fish, salt beef, and potatoes. But anyway, since we had no machinery they had to tow us into the [port] at Barbados. And then, it was an old-time sort of thing because we were unloaded by the stevedores who hadn't done this sort of thing for years. And they got into their West Indian songs; you know, when they're working, they're singing. And they unloaded us by hand. Then there was a period when the harbour masters, and so on, got together with the captain and said that with all that leaking they wanted the boat recaulked. So there was a period of caulking done.

And then we loaded barrels of rum and molasses for Halifax. And then we started back home. And it was still cold, it was not mid-summer. We sailed, had excellent going until we started to get into the cold weather having crossed the Gulf Stream.

And then one morning, the watch on deck heard a shot. And it was a U-boat over there which had fired a warning shot. So we all tumbled out. Couldn't see what it was, really. And eventually this—oh, what we're looking at fired another couple. Straddled us. In other words, stay there. And she kind of motored in and there was the swastika flying with the German flag up. We didn't have any doubts, then, what it was. She stopped about a quarter of a mile away. And Captain Jensen said, "Well, they're apparently going to shell us so we better get off." We went down to the submarine. We rowed [toward it] in a lifeboat. Yeah, we left the *Angelus* there. We had all our sails up and we just rowed over. (*Was there a command to do this, or did he just recognize that was the thing to do?*) Our captain decided that. Because he said if we stayed, maybe the next shell is going to hit us, start killing us.

So we went down to the submarine, the whole crew, everybody, in one lifeboat. Tumbled in. Captain Jensen and his dog. And we—when we got alongside the submarine—these young Nazis were bringing out belts of ammunition and loading up machine guns and kind of sighting you as if they were going to take your picture. And we were wondering, because the laws of naval warfare about that time had changed. It all started when, I think, a Polish destroyer machine-gunned the crew of a submarine that had got into trouble. I think Hitler said that from now on it was total war at sea. And then there were a good many cases of the Germans machine-gunning men in the water. Running through them, you know, fifty men swimming around. Run through them, machine-gun them, drop a depth charge. So we were there and wondering which category we were going to be in.

(*But you kept rowing toward them.*) We stopped. We were right there then. We were just looking up at them. They were just twenty feet away. The German captain came out and he spoke English. And he said, "Send your captain up." So Captain Jensen went up. And then the people on the submarine were interested to know if there was anything that could change their menu. Like any fruits, tropical fruits, or something. Bananas or something to change their menu. What was aboard, what could they get? And, so they weren't interested in what we had. (*They weren't interested in the rum?*) I guess the captain didn't want a barrel of rum on that submarine, and you can see the point there.

The captain was quite decent. He told Jensen, he said, "Look, we're within the air patrol radius here," and he said, "Either I have to take you people prisoners or I have to set you loose." He said, "I'm going to set you loose. You can go back to your boat, you have twenty minutes. If you want to get things."

Now the [official] transcript here said that Captain Jensen said, "No, we won't go back because the lifeboat was well stocked." That's not what he said, because the lifeboat was not well stocked. The lifeboat was very poorly stocked. The reason that we didn't go back is that we started back and as we're getting there we remembered that the sub captain had said twenty minutes and he's going to start to shell the ship. Fifteen minutes were gone and we're still not at the boat, at the *Angelus*. Captain Jenson said, "We're just going to get on in time to get blown up, so we just have to veer off and go."

So that's what we did. We just took off and rowed. Tried to see if we could rig up a sail. The boat was not equipped with a sail. So we took some spare oars and made some kind of a crude thing with a couple of canopies. And the nine men started off. We figured that we were between the north part of Bermudian waters and getting in toward the George's Bank area. But we were getting out of the Gulf Stream and into the cold weather.

(*Could you see what happened to the* Angelus?) Yeah, we watched her go down. (*When twenty minutes passed....*) Right on the dot they started her—well, right away. They didn't—it wasn't twenty-one minutes, it was right on schedule. And they started with their deck gun. And you could see every time, you could see a ball of smoke and wood flying around. So one hit the crap house on the stern and blew that up! The cook house. And then the *Angelus* started to catch fire in different areas. And she started to go down by the bow, and the last was the stern. She just slid under water. (*And that was it.*) Yeah. So we saw her, and here we are hundreds and hundreds of miles out in the Atlantic with practically no food or water.

All right. So we.... (*And no radio.*) No radio. (*No one knows you're there.*) No one knows we're there. (*And the submarine does not invite you aboard.*) No. (*So how many are you in this lifeboat?*) Nine. And a dog.

So we kind of waddled along for a few days. This is where I'm not sure of the dates..... (*It's not the dates so much. I want to find out what you men are saying to each other when you discovered you're in a bathtub hundreds of miles from anything—and nothing but the strength in your arms to get you....*) No, we weren't going to try and row because you couldn't row several hundred miles. And the boat only had about two oars anyway. So there was no question of rowing. We just hope somebody sees us and, meanwhile, we'll waddle along with this old sail as best we can. We knew we were going in the right direction—because Captain Jensen, he didn't bring any navigational instruments, but any seaman is able to look at Polaris, the North Star, and figure that America's gotta be over there somewhere, you know. You can head there or you can head there, you're going to get to America sooner or later.

(*What was the conversation....*) Oh, everybody was scared. We were scared. But we all were confident that we would be picked up. We told ourselves that anyway. (*Did you stop and pray?*) No. (*Anything like that?*) Well, that's going to come up in a few minutes, when the storm came up. (*Okay. You continue.*)

Well, the big storm came up. It started with swells that were so big. They were just—especially when you're in a lifeboat—just about this far from the water, a swell forty feet high can look like a bloody mountain. Not breakers—big, big rounded swells. No danger from them. It was just swells from a disturbance, probably, somewhere else in the Atlantic. That always happens at sea, you get swells. (*But no danger from that?*) Well, a lifeboat or even a small yacht can go through gigantic swells, but it's only when they break that you get in trouble.

So we were wondering about these swells—what's causing it? And we suffered from cold quite a bit. We were not properly dressed. I mean, it's just like you jumped over the side with what you have on or less. And we were all dressed up in any old crazy thing that you could find to wrap around you.

So this big storm came after the swells, and I believe we were approaching George's Bank. But the wind started to pick up, and it kept on picking up, and it kept on picking up. Captain had us put out a sea anchor, which is a canvas cone with oil in it. It didn't do any good. The sea anchor was to keep us heading into these, because the swells are stopping and now they're starting to turn into waves. Big roar from a breaking top of a wave, you know, a hell of a sound. And the storm kept building up, building up, building up.... Wind. And Captain Jensen was at the stern of the lifeboat...his little dog was always sitting in his lap. And he was steering away, been steering all day. And you could see him dropping off to sleep sometimes. Meanwhile I got some very bad cramps and I was all doubled up. And I remember one of the Newfoundland kids, they were boys, told Captain Jensen that he would relieve him and to try and lie down and get a little rest, and I did the same thing, steering the boat. And, anyway, we did that.

Sometime during the night, I'm not sure when, pitch black— and now we're in a storm. Great big waves, roaring and frightening hell out of you, and breaking. And all of a sudden, I remember here, seas are coming this way and we're going along with this. All of a sudden: up, up, up, over! (*Head over heel?*) Yeah. Not rolled over that way. (*Not rolling to the side.*) Big, big wave comes up under it and here she goes. Lifts the stern. She coasts down [the wave], digs her bow in the water, and over she goes. All men all over the place. Cold water—icy. The kind of water you die in, you know, in a few minutes.

When the boat was there upside down, we're all in the water, everybody's swimming back to clammer up on the boat or hold onto it. We were all hollering roll call. Who's here and who isn't. Captain Jensen didn't show up, or his dog. He was missing. We knew we wouldn't live long in that water—and we all got around on one side—and I still am amazed that we were able to do it—the boat capsized either four or five times within a couple of hours — and each time we were able to—either the seas rolled her over or, on one or two occasions, we had actually got down and helped her over, you know? And then we'd sit on the bottom. The boat's upside down sometimes. And certainly it's still being washed over by waves; we were in the water half the time. And this is when the hypothermia started to come in. And I can't remember at all except that, during that night, one after another of those guys just [drifted away]. Fall asleep, and that's how hypothermia works. Just fell asleep and fell over.

The final one is—when the boat was righted there were several men still alive in the boat, and she didn't turn over anymore....

So there were several men in the boat. You were asking about praying. So there I did see a couple of those boys, you know, making the sign of the cross.... There was no talking, loud praying or anything, but they were praying all right, and I was, too. In fact, I offered to become a deacon of the church at that time if the Lord would get me out. I promised him I would become a deacon, or a bishop, or anything. Just get me out of here. I didn't keep the promise.

So we had a gradually improving situation. (*As far as the weather.*) Yeah. We're down to maybe four or three men, something like that. And I remember two of them died. Two of the Newfoundlanders died very quickly, one after the other. In the boat. They just seemed to go to sleep. And one of them was Sandy, the son of the mate. The mate was holding him, trying to keep him warm—Sandy died in his arms, his son. And he wouldn't...holding him and just wouldn't let go of the boy. Because when these people would die we had to put them over the side. We couldn't have the boat floating with dead bodies all over the place.

So the mate didn't want to release his son and he held onto him until the next day. Now, by this time, the cook was at one end of the boat, [the mate] was at the other holding his son, and I was somewhere sitting around. And we went over to the mate and said, "You know, you have to let Sandy go." And he cried, and we put him over the side. So that [left] the mate, the cook, and myself.

Now, the boat was poorly stocked. It had some very inappropriate stuff. You don't want corned beef if you're dying of thirst. Had a few [cans] of those things. It didn't have any fishing equipment, no lights. It did have flares. But not a lifeboat stocked according to regulations at all. But what we did have: a few cans of tinned milk, some corned beef, and so on. And nothing to open the cans with, except a knife, of course. And I don't think there was any milk, there was no water at all. And we saw a couple of things floating one time—pieces of board—and scraped some little barnacles off and ate them. Oh, toothpaste, we ate. I remember that. We ate a tube of toothpaste. Little barnacles, that's all. Nothing else. Had no water. It was the water that really.... We were thirsty because of swallowing all the salt and everything, I suppose.

And [one day] I heard a kind of a rap, rap, rap, rap. The cook had thrown every single can over the side. He went mad. And with the last can, he jumped over. And that was—hypothermia does that. It gets you up here first. And, so anyway, that's the story of the well-stocked lifeboat—it wasn't. And the cook went out of his mind and threw the food overboard. So that left the mate and myself. That's all.

Nothing to fish with, and all sorts of fish around. There was a shark, a small shark, that circled the boat when we were on the bank. That was when [the mate] and I were alone. And he was, kind of, at one end and I was at the other like this, see this little shark went by. And then I remember one of the last mornings we were there I heard this tremendous fluttering and about fifty-thousand mackerel, or herring, went right over like a cloud right over the top of us. (*Over the boat!*) Yeah. And then, over here another big noise, and then a whale breaks. So there were fish all around but we had no way of getting them.

Now, at this point, since I've gone this far, I'm going to brag a little. You probably read [in the newspaper account] that [the mate] couldn't help himself very much and he praised Boudreau for bailing out the boat. Now I don't know—a lot of those Newfoundlanders were bigger and stronger than I was and I don't know why I was able to do it but I tore out, under the seat, I tore out a tank. We had a knife. And I sawed this tank in two, it was copper. A thin copper tank, not like anything that was steel or anything. So I hacked the end off it and bailed the boat out myself. And, I don't know, the mate and I kept warm by just wrapping up together in the bottom of the boat. And the weather turned very warm, and we were very thirsty and there was no water at all. And we, there was two mornings we did this, we felt around the deck and there was the morning dew—so we used to lick the seats just to get some water just to get rid of the parch.

Okay, I haven't got my days straight now, but anyway one day, or one evening at dusk, we hear a drone of an aircraft and we see this aircraft coming. This is a great coincidence and a very narrow chance, but got the flares. They had been under water. Struck them, no good. Struck, struck, struck them, no good. Finally, the last flare went PSSSH! Supposed to go for a full minute or more, just a little.... Right away that plane saw it and banked down. When he flew over us he wiggled his wings. We knew we were saved then. Because we knew we had been seen.

But [the mate] figured he had about another few hours to go, and I probably didn't have much better. Because at night we were both.... Oh, another thing I forgot to tell you, we lost our eyesight! He was at one end. I couldn't see him, he couldn't see me. And we were starting to have hallucinations. Because as a boy I had an uncle in Paragon Park. And I woke up one night and I could see the ferris wheel, and I could smell the hot dogs, popcorn. So I said, "Art, I know where we are! We're right off Paragon Park!" The next morning, of course, we weren't near Paragon Park, we were hundreds of miles out in the ocean.

So, at daylight the destroyer was right there. She was coming right down to us. The destroyer *Escort.* And she took us aboard. We were able to get up the net ourselves, both of us. I guess they may have reached and helped us, but they didn't carry us up or take us up in stretchers. And we were then wrapped up and taken good care of. And the cook brought down an enormous breakfast, and then came and took it away from us again. I was just getting ready to hoe into a bunch of bacon and eggs, and toast, and doughnuts. Somebody came down and said the doctor said to take that away from them right away.

All right, well, we're getting near the end. (*Well, when did they feed you?*) The doctor then said, "Here, you can have this. Then a little later, in an hour, you can have a little more." So after a while they gave us all we wanted of everything. Then the captain had us go up to his cabin and try and describe the submarine. Asked us where we thought we were, he showed us a chart. And the captain said, "Well, you're not too far off, you were fairly close." So he said, "We're going to go now and see if we can spot this submarine." So, we didn't head for shore then, but we were in good shape then. We were being taken care of. So off we went to look for the submarine. And then they couldn't find it so they brought us to Portland, Maine. That's it....

(*I guess you get off and you gave up sailing forever after that experience, right?!*) No way!... I didn't give it up at all. I only stopped sailing in 1990. (*At the age of....*) Well, I'm 74 now, so just about when I was 70, 71, I had to give it up. I didn't get fired but I was told that it was time to go and start a farm.

(*Walter, I really want to know what it was like to be in the black of that night in that lifeboat. There's eight or nine men with you, and seas forty feet high, and that boat flips. Here you are flying through the air on a dark night in a storm. What do you feel?*)

I don't know about the other guys, but I think what made me live when they couldn't was I didn't think I was going to die. And I was determined that I wasn't going to. And I remember sitting on the keel of that boat singing at the top of my lungs. And doing this to keep warm. (*Moving your arms back and forth, beating yourself.*) Yeah, and singing. You know, "Roll Out the Barrel," or whatever. Loud, loud, loud. But never thinking that I was going to die. And I think that's what the difference was between my mentality and, maybe, the guy next to me who said, "Oh, it's all over." That makes a big difference.

We had several of them singing. Loud singing. Loud. As loud as you could sing. So you can get the picture. A boat upside down, big waves, bunch of men out there singing "Roll Out the Barrel"!

(*To turn a boat over in water....*) Very heavy. I think that what we did, really, is we took advantage of a wave and helped the wave to turn it over, to roll it over. We couldn't do it alone. It had to be that the boat is almost going so we helped, and we just did the last teetering. But it happened five times, you see.

(*Was this the adventure you hoped to have on a square-rig?*) No. It's not what I had in mind!

Aboard the Wreck of the *Kismet II* at Meat Cove, 1955

The *Kismet II* was a 2,848-ton freighter that wrecked on the northern Cape Breton shore in November 1955. It was driven ashore in fierce winds, the hull ripped open by rocks, and twenty-foot waves made rescue by boat impossible. A convoy of vehicles headed out for the wreck. It took them seven hours from Sydney to Meat Cove, with a snowplow leading the way. After a long, hungry wait for the seventy-mile-an-hour winds to die down, the sailors were finally lifted off by a helicopter from Canadian Forces Base Shearwater. It was an heroic rescue close alongside that cliff wall, and it earned the George Medal for the helicopter's pilot and crew. That story starts on page 123.

After the *Kismet II* was abandoned and the crew were safe at the Navy League Seamen's Home in Whitney Pier, Sydney, John Angus Fraser of Meat Cove went on board.

Aboard the Wreck!
by John Angus Fraser

HERE'S ANOTHER CHAPTER of my life with my beautiful wife Ronie.

It was on the 27th of November, one real cold morning—and that time of the year you can get some pretty bad storms.

And on this said morning at six a.m. I woke Ronie and told her that I heard a moose bawling. You can just imagine how much Ronie loved me that morning to wake her, and I wanted her to come out of bed just because I heard a moose bawling. But I heard it again, and I got a feeling that she heard it, as she did come out on the verandah with me. We both stood on the verandah—looking so stupid at six a.m. in the morning, approximately 50-mile-an-hour gale and snowing. I know the way Ronie was looking at me she didn't like the idea. But sure enough, there it went again.

I looked at Ronie and said, "Now, Honey, wasn't I right? Isn't that a moose bawling?" "Well," Ronie said, "if it is a moose bawling, he is firing rockets out of his nose."

I looked up where she was pointing and there were the rockets going up around a hundred feet. And the moose bawling was distress calls from the ship, which meant a ship ashore—I could tell from where the rockets were coming over the mountain.

So I said to myself, "John Angus, here we go again." And it was really true, for the next couple of weeks we really went.

The first thing, the R.C.M.P. were called, and the rescue party, as it was so rough on the water that no ship could get near it. Then we all proceeded by land to where the ship was ashore. When we got overlooking the ship there was an approximately one-hundred-foot bank—sheer cliff—no possible way in the world to get anyone off by land. But we managed to pull some cables ashore by the ship's crew firing a rocket with a small cable, and pulling up a big one and anchoring it down. But that didn't help the crew any as the gale was pretty bad by then, and the wind was so heavy that a helicopter couldn't fly.

As I am writing this tonight the radio is on, and there's a song that just came on it ("Here Comes My Baby Back Again"). I'll tell you, that's the hardest thing in the world for me to take. It could be due to my writing this and thinking about Ronie, but it's hard for me to keep from breaking the radio, or running and putting my arms around it and kissing it. Because that is one of the songs Ronie and I were dancing to about five in the morning, when I returned from the *Kismet* loaded with whiskey. That morning we were still dancing, as the people were passing the house thought we were crazy—music going and us dancing at nine or ten in the morning. But I'll tell you more about that later.

How about more of the *Kismet*. But the *Kismet* is the *Kismet*. But everything odd happened in our life, like that ship the *Kismet*, it being from Europe, and millions of rocks further off the shore than the rock that the *Kismet* hit, and then drifted practically on our doorstep. And our house being the closest to the ship, as we are the last house in Meat Cove. On hitting this rock she lost her rudder and couldn't steer. But anyway, it made our house the centre of everything, as everyone coming and going would call in for lunch or information.

The ship was approximately three hundred feet, five thousand ton, a crew of thirty—twenty-eight men, one parrot, one budgie—headed for P.E.I. for a load of potatoes. No cargo aboard except lots of beer, and rum and whiskey—the strongest I ever drank, except my own homebrew.

Now to get those men off was the problem. The only way left was the helicopter, and with the wind blowing as hard as it was, that wasn't going to be easy. But around one in the afternoon the wind went down enough to lift the crew off [by helicopter], but definitely no equipment, as then it was so bad on the water that they couldn't let their own lifesaving boats down, and the pilot was scared that the wind would blow up again, and he would be blown against the cliff.

That was two-thirty, and it gets dark around four-thirty. At six o'clock crazy John Angus and a friend named Fraser went on one of the craziest, and stupidest, and dangerous adventures that I was ever on, and let me tell you it was crazy. Believe it: we headed out on that ocean that night—snowing, blowing—with a small two-bit flashlight, no graplin, two broken paddles and an eight-foot rowboat that was so old that nobody would go out in it during the summer. The last two people who had it out pulled it up on the beach and pulled it apart. Now, that not being their boat, they went to a lobster trap and took some half-inch nails out and stuck the plank back to the stern.

Fraser and I pushed it in the water to see if it was leaky, and it was not. But I found out later why it wasn't. Any old boat, no different how leaky it is, when the frost comes the water will freeze in the seams and form ice and won't leak again until the ice melts. And we proved that point the next day [when it was warmer] when we went to push it in the water—plunk!—it went right to the bottom, without anyone in it.

But as luck happened, there was no surf on Meat Cove Shore that night, as the westerly gale blows out Meat Cove River, and it's off land in the small bay of Meat Cove. But after you pass the western point of the cove of Meat Cove, then you get the wind.

Away we went for the *Kismet*. When we got there we couldn't find it. It was one of the darkest nights I ever remembered, and our light was so bad that you would practically have to be on top of something in order to find it. The first time we passed the *Kismet*, but the second try we picked it up. It was practically like the side of the mountain, as it stood so high out of the water. It went in on high tide, and the tide was low when we got there.

Now the wind dropped some—I should say it was after going down good. But there still was that long heavy roll, and running away up on the side of the boat, which made it impossible to get near it. So, we kept going along the side of the ship, with no intentions in the world to try and go aboard. But one of our trips along the side of her, we looked at a rope coming down from one of the lifesaving boats—a big rope practically as stout as your wrist. I told Fraser to row in to see if that rope was tied, for what reason I don't know.

So Fraser went in, I stood up in the bow of the boat, and I caught the rope and put my weight on it and away the boat went from under my feet, and there I was dangling in the air. So I said to myself, "John Angus, you better move." And move I did—up as fast as I could go. But every time I would get close to the boat, the rope would slip and down I would go. Sometimes I would go as far as my feet going in the water. Some more times I would go about half way. I tell you, I was getting tired and getting scared. I came to the conclusion that someone was still aboard, and was doing that to see if I would go back in the boat.

Where was the boat? There was no way for him to find me— the only light we had was the small light in my pocket. So the boat was out.

Eventually I made the lifesaving boat. I stayed there about ten minutes without moving. I mean, I couldn't move—I was too tired. When I got some of my strength back, I took out my flashlight and shone it around. I couldn't see anyone. Then I went in aboard the big ship, and I made a holler. And sure enough, someone answered me, but I couldn't tell where it was coming from.

Then I shone the light on the coil of rope, and my blood went cold, the hair stood up on the back of my neck. There wasn't a track [a footprint] around the coil of rope. There was around an inch or two of snow on the deck, and not a track anywhere. Then I walked over to the coil of rope to have a closer look at it, and there was nothing in the world that I could see that was keeping that rope in the coil. There's an explanation for everything, but Ronie's boy wasn't going to look for it then. Right then, along with the hair rising on the back of my neck and on the top of my head, there was a big yellow strip running down my back.

And right there and then, I thought I heard a movement behind me. Turning as fast as I could, something struck my hand and away went the light. Naturally the thought that went through my mind was that someone hit my hand in order to put out the light. John Angus backed up and kept backing up until something solid came against my back and there I stayed, for how long I can never tell.

And then everything started going through my mind. The first thoughts came to me that there was definitely someone aboard. And then it was hard to figure out, if there was someone aboard, where were the lights? And then I came to the conclusion that if there was really someone on ship, he was smuggling himself into Canada—maybe a murderer and maybe a dope smuggler. I thought of everything, and everything I was thinking of was worse than what I was thinking of before.

And then I started to listen to see if I could hear anything. And I am telling you I really started to hear things. I wish you were aboard of a ship rolling in a heavy sea against a cliff, so scared that your teeth were practically rattling. And you could hear that steel rubbing against each other. Now and again a door would slam open and closed. And I tell you, you can take two pieces of steel and start rubbing them together. And if you can rub them hard enough, you will swear to the God above that it's a bunch of people talking. Now you just imagine in my place—so dark, I'm sure if I would light a match it wouldn't show any light. I could hear that steel rubbing together, figuring that it was not one person but a bunch of them. Along with that, now and then you would hear a big bang—one of the big waves hitting the side of the ship, and the wind blowing through the rigging. And you froze with your back against something, and just waiting for those hands that knocked the light out of yours to creep around your neck. And that was not a nice feeling.

And I knew I had to move, as I was starting to get cold. So I made one big holler, which I had no intention of making. And sure enough, I got my answer. I still didn't know where it was coming from, but I knew it wasn't close to me. Then I got on my hands and knees and started to look for the flashlight. And sure enough, I got it, but it was broken. So I figured the best thing to do is try another holler to find out which deck they were on, the upper or lower. I got an answer again to my holler. Then I thought of my buddy and getting back aboard—maybe they wouldn't try and stop me—and if they did I could always jump.

So when I got to the railing, I hollered. And Fraser answered me, and nobody else. And I asked Fraser did he answer me every time I hollered. He said yes, the four times I hollered. Then I went back to the place I lost the flashlight, or got it knocked out of my hand. There was nothing knocked it out of my hand. When I swung around fast, my hand hit the guardrail on the stairs going to the upper deck, and away went the light. And I made one more holler, and when Fraser did answer, my mind was at ease.

Now another problem arose. If there were no human beings, what about the coil of rope? But I wasn't worried too much now. Just find a light. So I had some paper matches that weren't too good in the wind, and I would try not to light them until I would get inside of a door. The first door I went into sure took the wind out of me when I lit the match. When I lit the match I cupped it with my hands. And when you light a match like that, you are blinded for a second. And with that flash of the match and the small vision I had of that room—it was one of the most horrible things I ever laid eyes on. I never waited to light another match. I said to myself, "John Angus, what kind of ship is that?"—as what the glimpse of my eyes caught: parts of human bodies—their arms, their hips, their heads, their ribs. So I got out of that room fast.

Do you see the horror that I was going through? All because I like to be on some adventure, no different how wild it may be, or how crazy.

Aboard the *Kismet II*, 1955

I don't remember how I got on the bridge. When I came to myself I was in the officers' dining room. It was a beautiful room with a big table in the centre and about five half bottles of rum on it, which I found out later. And they were in a container that was attached to the table. But there was no light anywhere. The light I was looking for was lanterns. I know all the ships carry them in case of lights trouble. On another match I made the container with the rum in it. I got my hand around the quart, and drank about half of it. After that got down, I started to feel better. My knees quit knocking, and I was getting back quite a lot of pluck.

I was sitting there about five minutes when I thought I heard something behind me. I waited for a period, but there was no more noise. Then I lit another match and looked around the room. But there was nothing but a big wall clock and a stuffed parrot on it. My pluck was coming back again. I turned around to the table, reaching my hand out to get another bottle, when this fellow spoke from behind me, gently first. I couldn't speak even if I tried, as I figured, "This is really it." I got my hand on the bottle. I was a little happier: I had a weapon, and a ghost don't talk. I didn't know what he said, as I knew it was a Greek ship and I didn't understand their language. Just as I was leaving the door, he really came down on the language he was using. But then I really had to find a light.

So I kept on searching. I can take an oath on the Bible that I never went in and out of so many doors in my life. But I found out in the daylight there was only about ten doors. I'd been going in and out the same doors all the time. But I found a lamp first, and then when I got that lit I found a flashlight. But later on when I went through those rooms [I found out that] there were lamps and flashlights in every room except two. And I think I was going in and out of those same two rooms all night. And when I looked again at that bottle I drank half out of, I know why I was going in and out those same two rooms!

Now I had two lights and my head was after clearing some. But I was still loaded. I was really plucky then, I was going back to tackle that fellow that stopped me from my drinking that beer, even if he was old pirate Blackbeard. Away I went. I was actually singing, not a care in the world. That is, until I got to the door of the dining room. When he heard me coming he started to sing, or at least I thought he was. But when I flashed the light around the corner, he started with that wicked language again. Drunk or not I was still scared. But on flashing the light around the room there was nobody in the room. Boy, that was confusion! I said to myself, "John Angus, you are crazy or you are dealing with an invisible man." I kept going to the table for another drink. And I needed the drink then.

But when I got to the table I heard this invisible person talking behind me. I turned around and still couldn't see anyone, and that stupid person just kept on talking. First time, I was too frightened, and this second time I was too drunk. And when I started to drink out of the next bottle, it sobered me up real fast. This bottle had something in it to sober the crew up fast in case they were needed.

Sitting down on the chair or whatever was there to sit on, for no reason, I looked up at the clock, and there was a flicker of movement caught my eye. I was after sobering up then—I mean, my head was clearing—because I came to the conclusion that there was no invisible man. Perhaps it was someone in the captain's quarters on a loudspeaker system, or a radio still [further] on somewhere.

That's when I saw the movement. I actually was looking for the loudspeaker. I went over to the clock and reached up to catch the stuffed parrot. Well, my heart was stopping and going all night, and this time it really stopped. Just when I was catching the parrot, it made one screech and flew away. You just imagine! With all the time I was frightened out of my life that night, and then to reach up with the intentions of catching a stuffed parrot, and him to screech in your face. You can believe it, I had a flash of the other world, my heart stopped that long.

Now there I was, surprised, happy, and mad. So me and that parrot really went at it. If someone had a movie camera on, you would think we were dancing. Every time my fingers would just about touch the parrot he would fly away to another place in the room. And then I would go after him again, staggering and tripping over everything. And he would just about let me put my fingers on him before he would move. And around and around that room he and I would go.

Why I mentioned the word dancing—thinking back, I believe

that bird was singing. And instead of flying directly to his object, he was actually rocking in the air. Of course, that could account for what I had out of that bottle. So I let him be, figuring that the next time there I would catch him and take him home for Ronie.

Now, leaving that room, and out on deck again, I said, "John Angus, everything is turning out so good. Go back and have a look at all those human arms and legs and hips and everything that I saw crazy in that room. If it's dead it can't hurt anyone." And I proved it was dead, believe it. It was their storage room: parts of beef, parts of practically every animal you would want to eat. It was also their freezer.

And then, boy-oh-boy, my eyes popped. Behind all the edible stuff they had the drinking stuff. And I don't mean pop and milk—the best of spirits, and tons of beer. I figured I could take it all. And then I thought of the old boat we had with us. And then I thought of my friend Fraser. Fraser—his engine could break down and he would be in pieces on the shore. I mean his broken paddles could break worse, which would be the same.

When I got back to the railing I started to holler. And he was a half mile away from the ship, as it started to snow and he couldn't see anything. So he went astray in the snow squall. He was so far away that he couldn't hear me holler, but I heard him holler. He was on the windward side of me, and he saw the light and started to holler.

Now, while he was coming back to the ship, I started to take out some beer, but mostly rum and whiskey. I think we got aboard eight cases of rum and some cases of beer. I'm not sure of the other things we put aboard. But I can assure you it was too much load for the boat. I found a small rope and lowered all the stuff down from the lifesaving boat. And when Fraser said she was loaded, I was trying to think of some present to bring home for Ronie. I would love to get the parrot, but that was out. I knew if I went back he would want to dance. And by that time I was getting a headache. There was something else in my mind, and then I thought of it—the budgie. And he was in his cage, and I knew he would not fly around. But in which of those two or three hundred rooms did I see him?

So I told Fraser I would be back in a short while. Then I went on my hunt, but no find. Then I thought that it was just one of those crazy things that I had been seeing. And then another thought came into my mind: I never remembered being into the steering room of the ship, which would be the most fascinating room of the ship. When I found it, there was the budgie, a nice camera, and a nice field glass. The camera was another present for Ronie. Until today, I am wondering if I didn't imagine that budgie being on that ship, because I definitely couldn't forget that room, with the big steering wheel all brass, and the big compass all brass—practically the room was made of windows and brass. What I mean, I remembered everything that was in the other rooms, but never remembered seeing that room, and still I previously saw the budgie.

Then I thought of Fraser again. The boat could start leaking, and he couldn't bail it, as the best he could do is keep the boat off the rocks with the load in it, with two broken paddles. But when I got back to the lifesaving boat I could hear the singing, and the song he was singing—"What Would You Do with a Drunken Sailor?" And he sure was a drunken sailor, and now a drunken captain, as he was the captain of that little boat with those two broken paddles. Then he tried to pick me up, but no way. Every time I would go down on the rope, Fraser wouldn't be there. Then I would climb that rope again. And every time I would ask him why wasn't he under me, he would say that when he would get so close he couldn't see me, and my voice would be in a different place every time I would speak. And then he started to beg me to jump in the water and he would pick me up. You just imagine—to jump in that cold water. I told him Ronie's boy wouldn't think of that.

Well, he told me there was nothing he could do, unless I would let down the gangplank—the ladder on the side of the ship. And he just said it for a joke, but I didn't take it for a joke. Back aboard the big ship I went, tripped the big hauling winch, and away goes the side ladder. Luck happened he wasn't close to it. The sea that ladder made when it struck the water would have sunk the small boat.

But anyway, he picked me up in style. When I got in the little boat it was half full of water. Later on he told me he never thought of the water in the boat, and by that time he was up to his knees in it. I started to bail the boat when we left the *Kismet* and never stopped until we got to Meat Cove beach. And I was bailing twice as fast by the time I got to the shore. I know now the ice was melting. But we were two happy boys when we got ashore.

And much more happier when I got home in Ronie's arms, as that girl sure was worried, us leaving to go up and just have a look at the *Kismet* at approximately four in the evening. And then it was around four in the morning. I just couldn't believe it—where was I all that time? But she forgave me when I gave her the camera and the budgie, which was practically scaring Fraser to death by that time, as he was drinking some of that strong spirits.

Then the fun started. We had a few good drinks, and turned on the gramophone, listening to the music. But after a few more drinks we started waltzing, and when daylight came we were still waltzing, and the music turned away up. And all the people walking up to see where the *Kismet* went ashore, as the gale was after springing up again as soon as the sun started coming up. Now, nobody in the world knew or would believe that I got aboard that ship, and those people that were passing figured that Ronie and I were celebrating the ship going ashore.

It blew all that day, but the following day it was calm. Then Fraser and I headed back up again. And we couldn't see any boats around the *Kismet*, but they were there. They came from everywhere, from miles away. Now when Fraser and I climbed the ladder, what a beautiful sight: everyone dancing and singing songs, with a quart of rum in their hand. And every boat left that ship with all it could carry, mostly hard liquor. And when someone would heave a case overboard, which they could reach down and pick it up as the water was only shallow, they would say, "The heck with it, lots more aboard!"

And on that trip I went looking for the parrot. But when I found him he was dead. Someone was trying to catch him, and must have hurt him. And when I told Ronie she cried practically all day, because she really wanted that parrot....

[The next day] it was a beautiful afternoon, and Ronie and I could see all the boats, practically from everywhere, passing Meat Cove. And we knew that they were going to the *Kismet*. I figured that I should take another trip up. I knew that that day everything good and bad would come off. But the surprising thing was, when I turned the point in Meat Cove, every one of them was drifting around outside of the *Kismet*. When I got there the first person that I talked to was Johnnie Edmond. I asked him was he aboard, and the reply he made, "You would have to be a bird in order to get aboard. The R.C.M.P. came and pulled all the ladders up." Then I told Johnnie the R.C.M.P. couldn't do that as that was my ship, I was the first person aboard after the crew left it, and it was floating. But how to get aboard was another problem.

So in we goes. I took a cod jig and fired it up over one of the bars that was coming from the big ship to the small lifeboat. Kept pulling the cod line until I got a rope over the bar, then put a running knot on the rope, and away I goes. Ten minutes later every ladder was down. Twenty minutes later everyone was aboard. Thirty minutes later everyone was loaded—another big party aboard the ship. The only thing was missing was the girls for dancing, but we were dancing pretty good together.

Everyone left with all their boats could take. We couldn't take much. We only had small rowboats, and two and three of us in every boat. But we managed our liquor. Up until today, approximately fourteen years later, we are finding buried rum and whiskey....

This year—fourteen years later—Mr. S. G. MacLellan, my wife Ronie's father, was putting a basement under his house, and the house is approximately forty feet long. And he couldn't get jacked enough to lift the house. So he made a remark: When he would get the house up there would be enough liquor under there from the *Kismet* to get everyone in the country drunk. The next day there were enough people there to lift the house and hold it up until he got the blocks under it. And the liquor?

[More and more people went aboard the *Kismet II*. They came from all around Cape Breton. Joe Curtis of Bay St. Lawrence said that when they would be out lobster fishing, it seemed that "you just couldn't pass her without going aboard again." As an example, he took off thirty-five cans of paint, towed them away in the ship's own lifeboat. The *Kismet* was so completely stripped that when a salvage crew from Halifax arrived, they found virtually nothing left but the shell of the ship. It was a marvelous example of salvage, and of recycling!

Aboard the *Kismet II*, 1955

Brass pipes became drainpipes. Clocks and barometers and valves found new homes. Even the anchor chain was gone.]

The Heroic Rescue of the Crew of the *Kismet II*

$\mathbf{F}$ROM VARIOUS REPORTS, here's what happened to the crew of the *Kismet II*—the 2,848-ton freighter en route from Philadelphia to Summerside, P.E.I., filling with water, its lights and power gone.

HALIFAX HERALD, November 26, 1955

Her battery and generator gone dead and her holds gradually filling with water, the grounded Liberian freighter *Kismet II* wallowed barely 50 feet from razor-edged rocks off the northern tip of Cape Breton...as heavy navy trucks with breeches buoy gear and experts to use it raced to the scene.

The trucks left Sydney around 8:30 p.m. and had to make a 150-mile trip to Cape St. Lawrence with emergency highway crews plowing the road ahead of them.

An emergency message was sent to ham radio operator Mel Smith on the scene to have horses, bulldozers, tractors and all available men ready to clear a mile of path to the top of the cliff where rescue operations will be spearheaded....

Smith of ham station Ve1AO reported [the *Kismet II*] to be directly under an overhanging cliff which slopes downwards at an angle making rescue operations almost impossible....

Earlier in the day a Navy 'copter tried to contact the freighter but was unsuccessful. Lt. Cmdr. Roger Fink, co-pilot of the helicopter, said three lines were dropped to the ship and two reached. But because of the slope in the cliffs rescue was impossible.

"It would be difficult if not impossible to get a man up this incline," [said Fink]. "At one time we were showing 60 miles per hour, and we weren't moving an inch...."

Ham operator Smith has been on the scene since 7:15 a.m. Friday

123

with portable radio equipment. He was able to drive a jeep and trac-tor right to the edge of the cliff and relay messages to his wife, Kay Smith, ten miles away, [who] then relayed to ham operator Bob Wicks in Sydney and messages reached Halifax via regular communication lines.

Smith reported he couldn't see the ship earlier in the morning be-cause of the overhanging ledge and heavy snow. He said later he could see some of the 28 [actually 21] crew members scampering about the ship....

The cliffs, he said, were covered by about six inches of wet, sticky snow....

Early this morning efforts were being made by the RCMP rescue teams on the scene to lower walkie-talkies to the boat. Winds were re-ported up to 35 miles per hour....

Most of the day, [Smith said] waves were breaking over the ship's mast pushing it further into the shore.

The only avenue the crew of the stricken ship have now of evacua-tion is by rope up the cliffs or in small boats. This last resort was be-lieved here to be almost impossible during the present weather conditions.

It is hoped that the breeches buoy equipment can be rigged from the clifftop to the shore so the crew can be...plucked from the ship in the basket-like chair that travels along the rope from shore to shore.... Experts who will manage the breeches equipment...were flown by RCAF from Halifax last night to Sydney but the plane could go no fur-ther due to the weather.

Off shore, the tanker *Gulfport* had been standing by but the weather forced her to leave.

FROM A NAVY MAGAZINE

The breeches buoys, lines and other rescue equipment was transferred to a truck.... Headed by a snow plow, the convoy started over the Ca-bot Trail. They were stopped short of their goal by narrow mountain roads, covered with ice, and small, unsafe bridges. The journey had to be completed on foot....

Meanwhile, the crew of the *Kismet II* were cold, wet, their food ruined—into their second day trapped on the rocks at the foot of the cliff. Helicopter pilot Roger Fink later remembered: "Although of Liberian registry the crew were all Greek seamen. The First Mate could speak English and told us that the pounding waves ground the hull continuously onto the rocks. His primary concern had been to prevent the men attempting to swim ashore after they had lost the one usable lifeboat....

"Due to a cliff overhang it was not possible to get into a position above the masts, booms and other top hamper so a hoist rescue was ruled out."

An unsuccessful attempt was made to reach the ship by helicopter that first day.

FROM THE NAVY REPORT

Lt. Cdr. Beeman was not long in learning that the gale, blowing parallel to the cliff, had created terrific air turbulence. As it flew shoreward, the helicopter suddenly dropped about 500 feet, almost to the waves, and just as suddenly was tossed aloft again. Any effort to approach the ship could only result in the machine being smashed against the cliff face or thrown into the sea.

The helicopter returned to Sydney. Next morning, rested, they returned to the *Kismet*. The wind was still blowing at from 25 to 45 knots, but it had shifted slightly, perhaps not more than 10 degrees, though there was a chance there might be relatively smooth air near the ship in the lee of the cliff.

Lt. Cdr. Beeman made a test run close to the surface and found that this conjecture was true and he hovered near the stern of the ship while his crew indicated by chopping motions with their hands that they wanted a landing space cleared. The seamen flew to work with axes, saws and hammers, chopped down the after binnacle, ripped away the guard rails and in five minutes had cleared the poop deck of all top hamper.

The helicopter slipped in sideways and touched three wheels to the deck, balancing there with power on. Four fingers were held up to indicate the number of passengers which could be taken. "You could count in seconds the time it took the men to get aboard," Lt. Cdr. Beeman said afterward. "They were in like jack-rabbits."

That was trip No. 1, and Lt. Cdr. Fink and PO Vipond were left behind at Bay St. Lawrence to make more room on the next attempt. This time they signaled for six sailors to get aboard, but when they were airborne, the helicopter seemed unusually sluggish and a count of heads showed that a seventh had scrambled in. Lt. Cdr. Fink and AB Smith made the third trip, bringing back six of the *Kismet* crew. Lt. Cdr. Fink also piloted the fourth and final trip, with PO Vipond accompanying him.

This brought off the remaining four men, the captain's dog and, it was discovered on land, the ship's cat as well....

"During the 30 hours on the rocks," [said Captain Anast Maniatis, of Athens, Greece] "I felt we were in danger at all times. I am most thankful the pilot was able to come in this morning because I knew that if the wind shifted again rescue would be impossible." A short time later the wind did shift and that night a fierce storm laid more inches of snow on the ground.

Roger Fink said: "Jack Beeman and I received the George Medal while Lawrence Vipond and Paul Smith were each awarded the Queen's Commendation for this combined effort. [The George Medal, presented by the Queen, is an award "for acts of bravery...intended primarily for civilians and...military services...confined to actions for which purely military honours are not normally granted."] In addition to the 21 men, one dog and a cat [rescued from the *Kismet II*], the last sailor to board the helicopter brought off a coal scuttle filled with bottles of Four Star Hennessey Cognac and we each got a 26 of that!"

HALIFAX HERALD

On its return journey to Shearwater the Sikorsky helicopter which accomplished the rescue operation, ran out of fuel and emergency tanks had to be rushed to it at North River Bridge at St. Ann's Bay. After refueling further at Sydney, it started on its homeward trek....

Notes

Journal of the Voyage and Wreck of the *Auguste*, 1761

The remains of the *Auguste* were discovered in 1977 by diving teams headed by Eddie Barrington and Bob MacKinnon.

But who was Saint-Luc de la Corne?

The following is from an essay by Dr. G. G. Campbell, a noted local historian and extremely influential principal of Sydney Academy. Left unfinished at his death, it was to be an introduction to a book that would have included Saint-Luc's *Journal*. We are pleased to be able to present Dr. Campbell's translation of the *Journal* in this book. And here is a portion of his essay:

Saint-Luc de la Corne

Luc de la Corne, Sieur de Chapts et de St. Luc, was born in Trois Rivieres [Contrecoeur] in 1711, the fifth of eight sons, seven of whom reached manhood. Saint-Luc, as he will be known here, lived in memorable times. (Note: In formal usage, De la Corne Saint Luc, or Saint-Luc de la Corne. In documents the man is often called Saint-Luc and this form is used here, since it is short and marks the man out from his brothers, several of whom played parts in the affairs of the time.) Rather more than half his adult life he spent in a Canada that was either actively at war, or in a state of armed and uneasy peace with Britain and Britain's colonies. Then, at the age of fifty, he chose to accommodate himself to life under British rule. He had some success in this, for he was appointed to Quebec's first Legislative Council, and lived to march with a British army against Britain's rebellious colonies. The shipwreck [of the *Auguste*, 1761] in which he suffered, described in the *Journal*, was at once a dramatic ending to the first phase of his eventful life, and a prelude to his life as a British subject.

For all he lived through stirring events, Saint-Luc is like a bit player, appearing now and then on stage without much affecting the action of the play. At odd moments he is centre stage; then he is off in the wings. His name occurs here and there in documents of the period, sometimes in relation to events of more than passing interest and significance. Then he is lost to view, and nothing is known of his current activities. But from bits and pieces, and especially from the *Journal*, there emerges the portrait of a hardy and resourceful man, quick to adapt to environment and circumstance, determined and ruthless, not always admirable but invariably interesting.

Saint-Luc's father held the post of Town Major, first at Trois Rivieres, then at Montreal. In these two places the boy spent his early years, though he probably finished his formal education in Quebec City, as was customary with children of the Canadian *noblesse*. He got an education of a different kind in the world of savagery that everywhere hemmed in French Canada. He learned Indian languages and Indian customs, came to be known by the Indians and to have influence with them. He was enrolled in the militia in 1734, held the rank of lieutenant in 1748, that of captain in 1758. But in both King George's War and the Seven Years War, he was known mainly in his role of partisan leader of the Indians. Indeed, he was commonly called "General of the Indians." Montcalm, in one of his sarcastic asides, refers to him as "King of the Indians."

In the outlying settlements of New England and New York, the name of Saint-Luc came to be held in fear and loathing. Of the reasons for this, no full account can be given. For the grim warfare in which he was active was waged in backwoods clearings, by small bodies of Indians and Canadians, and went often unreported. The raiding parties that sprang from the forest left a record of a kind, but it was an unwritten record of death and devastation. Only a chance reference here and there makes it clear that Saint-Luc earned well his reputation as a partisan fighter—and with it the hatred and fear of settlers in the hinterland of England's colonies.

Certain exploits in which he played a part are reported with some fulness. In the summer of 1756, he and a body of Indians assisted at the capture and destruction of the English forts at Oswego. Later in the year he was at Fort Carillon, known to the English as Ticonderoga, and the centre for raiding activities against settlements in New England and New York. Parkman likened the place to a hornets' nest, "pouring out swarms of savages to infest the highways and byways of the wilderness." In the early summer of 1757, the fort was the mustering place for the army that General Montcalm was to lead against Fort William Henry. Saint-Luc was a prominent figure in this expedition; some of its details are worth recalling for the light they seem to throw on an obscure passage in the *Journal.*

Notes

Fort William Henry stood at the southern end of the long waterway formed by the Richelieu, Lake Champlain and Lake George. By this route there was easy passage from the valley of the St. Lawrence to the valley of the Hudson. Fourteen miles from the fort, on the Hudson itself, stood another stronghold known as Fort Edward. In the spring of 1757, both forts were in English hands.

In a summer campaign, Montcalm planned to wrest the forts from the British and to secure control for France of the all-important waterway. For the purpose he had some 8000 troops, in part regulars from France, in part Canadian militiamen. And in ragged and undisciplined support of this army trooped a party of 1600 Indians under the immediate command of Saint-Luc de la Corne.

Forty-one Indian tribes were represented in that raucous and turbulent horde. Warriors from beyond the Mississippi were there, others from regions bordering the Atlantic. A war party of Micmacs had come from Nova Scotia. Watching their heathen antics, Bougainville, Levis and other officers new from France found them a hellish legion, foul in habit, undisciplined, treacherous, vicious, cruel. Some tribes boiled and ate their prisoners, and all rejoiced in inflicting torture. The conventions of civilized war, honoured by Montcalm and his officers, had no meaning for the Indians. They would use in war every savagery that fiendish ingenuity could devise. And once unleashed and about the business of bloodletting, they were incapable of being controlled. Saint-Luc knew this from lifetime experience; Montcalm was to learn it in the melee that followed on the capture of Fort William Henry.

The Fort was garrisoned by 2,200 British troops and contained as well the usual assortment of camp-followers, including women and children. Early in the siege, Saint-Luc and his Indians were detached to cut communications with Fort Edward, thus making it impossible for reinforcements to come through. The garrison held out for nearly a week, and then surrendered with honours of war and on terms that provided for its safe-conduct to Fort Edward. Pending arrangements for the march to Fort Edward, the inmates of the fort were moved to a fortified encampment near by. Whereupon the Indians, intent on plunder, penetrated the fort and slaughtered some wounded that had been left behind. During a confused and anxious afternoon, Montcalm and the French officers restored a semblance of order. A body of troops under Saint-Luc and other Canadian officers was posted to safeguard the

British encampment. An uneasy quiet fell with the darkness, but Indians were everywhere on the move. In the early morning, the incident described below, in the words of one of the survivors, set off a day of panic and butchery. Miles Whitworth, surgeon in the British garrison, deposed under oath

"...that the said Whitworth saw the French Indians about 5 o'clock in the Morn of the 10th of August dragg the said seventeen Wounded men out of their Hutts murder them with Tomohawks and scalp them

"that the French troops posted round the lines were not further than forty feet from the Hutts where the said wounded Men lay

"that several Canadian officers particularly one Lacorne were present and that none, either Officer or Soldier, protected the said wounded men."

After this, there was no holding the Indians. The British fled in panic along forest trails in the direction of Fort Edward, with the Indians in pursuit. Many hundreds were taken captive, a great many were killed and scalped. Appalled at the Indian violation of their military code, Montcalm and his officers risked their very lives in attempting to protect their prisoners; by their actions they saved many. But Saint-Luc and the Canadian officers seem to have made no attempt to stem the avalanche. [Editor: And while the trophy-taking of the Indians made many of de la Corne's contemporaries indignant, Governor Vaudreuil felt it merited him the Cross of Saint-Louis. Vaudreuil wrote: "This captain has rendered very fine service at all times...particularly in this last campaign at Carillon, having been at the head of a detachment that laid an ambush on the road to Fort Lydius in which he completely vanquished an enemy convoy." La Corne was made a Knight of Saint-Louis.]

Three years after the events described above, Saint-Luc wrote his *Journal*. He wrote, not for French eyes but for those of British officers then in the seats of power in New York, Quebec and Montreal. In a cryptic passage, he notes that the Micmac Indians who rescued him in his extremity recognized in him one whom they had known before, and who had been of service to them. Now there is no record of Saint-Luc's having visited Nova Scotia before his shipwreck. On the other hand, Micmacs are known to have been at Fort William Henry. Under the circumstances, Saint-Luc's unwonted reticence can perhaps be understood. The men who were to read his *Journal* had their own vivid recollections of what took place at Fort William Henry.

The capture of Fort William Henry was the last notable success of French arms in America. It is true that in the following year Montcalm successfully defended Fort Ticonderoga against a British army greatly superior in numbers to his own. But Louisbourg was taken in the east, and in the west the British secured control of Lake Ontario. In 1759, Quebec fell to the forces of General Wolfe. And in 1760, three armies converged on Montreal and forced its capitulation, thus ending the struggle for Canada.

During these years Saint-Luc was active in the field, but just where it is not always possible to say. Hostilities were conducted over a wide area, and there was much skirmishing and small-scale forest fighting. Governor Vaudreuil asserts in 1758 that Saint-Luc had served in all campaigns and "had always distinguished himself, especially at Carillon." Even while Wolfe was making upriver towards Quebec, Saint-Luc was with a mixed force of Indians and French at Oswego, where the British were rebuilding the fort destroyed three years earlier. This time, the French forces were repulsed, and Saint-Luc was wounded. He was back in action a year later when he was in command of a force posted at the head of the Long Rapids above Montreal. General Amherst was preparing to move his army downriver to Montreal, and the French force was to harass it in its passage of the rapids. The army came down without interference, and Montreal was soon in British hands.

The Articles of Capitulation that ended the struggle stipulated that officers and men from France were to be repatriated on British vessels. French Canadians who wished to do so were to be free to leave the country. Saint-Luc and an older brother, known as Chevalier de la Corne, were among those who decided to go to France.

[The two] spent the year following the Capitulation on the family seigneury at Terrabonne, not far from Montreal. Then, when arrangements for the voyage were completed, they made their way to Quebec and sailed on the *Auguste*. What happened thereafter is related in the *Journal*.

In 1742, Saint-Luc had married Marie Anne Hervieux, daughter of a prominent citizen of Montreal. By her he had four sons and three daughters. In the year of Louisbourg's capture, the mother having died, two of the boys were sent to France, presumably to complete their education. The ship in which they sailed was attacked at sea by the British, and the two boys perished. When Saint-Luc sailed on the *Auguste*, he had with him his two remaining sons. A brother, Abbé de la Corne, a prominent churchman resident in France, had secured for his nephews the necessary patents of nobility, and the boys were to have enrolled in a military school. Instead, they ended their young lives on a beach in North Cape Breton.

It may have been the loss of his sons that determined Saint-Luc to remain in Canada. The demonic urge that drove him on his great trek may have sprung from parental anguish. Whatever the cause, he could not rest until he was back on the St. Lawrence. There in Old Canada, that in important respects was strangely New, he found that for the Canadian *noblesse* conditions under British rule were not altogether uncongenial. As a matter of policy, the men who now ruled in Montreal and Quebec City were at pains to conciliate this important class, and to reconcile it to British rule. Saint-Luc seems to have settled easily into his new role as British subject....

Saint-Luc de la Corne died at his residence on Rue Saint-Paul in Montreal, October 1, 1784; he was buried October 4 in the chapel of Sainte-Anne in the church of Notre-Dame. His third wife lived on for another thirty-five years.

In 1761, the seven survivors of the wreck of the *Auguste* were saved by Mi'kmaw Indians who discovered them on the Jersey Cove beach across St. Ann's Bay from today's Englishtown, Victoria County. In 1780, nineteen people came off the wreck of the *St. Lawrence* near Margaree Harbour, and began a struggle in winter over the northernmost part of Cape Breton. Nine of these survived to reach that same spot at Jersey Cove beach. Their leader, Ensign Prenties, later wrote their story—it became known as "Ensign Prenties' *Narrative*."

As G.G. Campbell wrote: "The two narratives [Saint-Luc's and Prenties'] are linked by a strange coincidence. The family of Indians that rescued Prenties and his comrades had, nearly twenty years before, saved the lives of the men who survived the wreck of the *Auguste*. Even Prenties' pedestrian prose does not wholly obscure the drama of the scene in which this is made known. In the squalor of an Indian wigwam, Prenties relates in broken French something of the weeks-long ordeal he and his friends experienced. The story is relayed in Micmac to an attentive ring of Indian faces. Then an ancient woman, much moved by his recital, rises in her place and calls to mind the wreck of the *Auguste*. And she and her interpreter tell the old story of death and rescue for the edification of the broken and wasted men who themselves are enduring a hard, hard odyssey."

Ensign Prenties' *Narrative* of the 1780 wreck, and an 1823 shipwreck narrative by Samuel Burrows, are available as *Castaway on Cape Breton*, Breton Books, ISBN 1-895415-00-4.

Wreck of the *Astraea* at Little Lorraine, 1834

H. W. Crawley's report was found in late Provincial Archivist D. C. Harvey's article which appeared in *The Dalhousie Review*, 1941. A portion was published in *Cape Breton's Magazine* with the permission of Miss Margaret Harvey.

D. C. Harvey wrote that the wreck of the *Astraea* at Little Lorraine Head, Cape Breton, in 1834 "was one of the most tragic of the many shipwrecks that took place in the second quarter of the nineteenth century, when migration from the British Isles to the British North American colonies was in full swing, and unscrupulous ship-masters overcrowded their far-from-seaworthy craft to profiteer in human misery. For the first decade of this period there was not a lighthouse on the entire coast of Cape Breton Island, and, during that decade, on an average five ships a year were stranded between Louisbourg and Cape North, to be pillaged of their cargo or scattered far and wide as a menace to navigation.... It was these incidents, together with the tragic details of the wreck of the *Astraea*, which led the provincial government to appoint superintendents of shipwrecks for the northeastern and southeastern shores of Cape Breton, to keep constant lookout for such wrecks from Louisbourg to Scatarie and from Sydney to St. Paul's and to take prompt steps for their assistance....

"In 1836, the British government offered to erect lighthouses on St. Paul's and Scatarie Islands, if Lower Canada and the three Maritime Provinces would cooperate in defraying the expense of maintenance and administration. In the following year the four provinces reached an agreement, their respective legislatures appropriated the amounts agreed upon, and construction was undertaken forthwith.... [After] 1839, when the lights began to shine from St. Paul's Island and Scatarie, both the number of wrecks and the loss of life in those that occured diminished rapidly, while the way of the plunderer was made hard...."

Our thanks to Mike Delaney, with encouragement from John Flannigan, both of Sydney, who continued to search for information about the *Astraea*. They found the letter written by one of the three survivors, and sent it with a list of the names of every man, woman and child aboard that ill-fated vessel. We offer here the survivor's letter . The list of names has been deposited at the Beaton Institute archives at the University College of Cape Breton.

A North Sydney Harbour Tragedy, 1874
This story by Elva Jackson, an important Cape Breton historian, first appeared in the *Cape Breton Post*, 1957, and in a slightly different form, in her book *Window on the Past: North Sydney*. She is the author of *Cape Breton and the Jackson Kith and Kin* and several shorter works.

Wreck of the *Ariadne*, 1896
Lillian Crewe Walsh was a poet and ballad maker. See her "The Wreck of the *John Harvey*" on page 71. She is remembered by Cape Bretoners as the author of such poems as "The Ghost of Bras d'Or," "Kelly's Mountain," and "The Lady of the Loom"—the latter being the poem that inspired the Cape Breton Tartan. We found this story in manuscript form in a trunk of her papers. We went to Neil's Harbour to photograph the communion chalice and the graves of the men of the *Ariadne* who were buried in the churchyard. We met the Rev. David Reid, then Rector of St. Andrew's Church, who gave us information on the wreck of the *Ariadne* included in our introduction. As shown in the photo section, a granite monument now replaces the original wooden cross.

The Inquiry into the *Dorcas* and the *Etta Stewart*, 1893
This article is based on Michael MacDonald's reading of the newspapers, local memories, and his own search along the shores and in several cemeteries. Michael is an innkeeper in Louisbourg.

Wreck of the *Watford* at Schooner Pond, 1932
Author Sara MacLean was for many years a librarian in Glace Bay.

The Wreck of the *Hurry On* near Judique, 1935
Euphemia Malcolm MacEachern's poem was first found in the collection of the Beaton Institute, University College of Cape Breton. News-

papers used could not always be identified, but the passages quoted here come principally from the *Halifax Herald* and the *Halifax Chronicle*.

Fishermen Rescue American Seamen at Louisbourg, 1943

The main body of this story was written by Jean Kyte, an indefatigable researcher in Louisbourg. Her entire article was first published in *The Coastal Courier*. To this edited version of her article are added portions from conversations with two of the fishermen involved in the rescue.

Walter Boudreau: Louisbourg Rescue, and *Angelus*, 1943

On the boardwalk in Louisbourg, August 24, 1996, the Louisbourg Heritage Society unveiled a memorial plaque to the two sets of men who rescued the *S.C. 709* crew. Ed Levy and Walter Boudreau were present.

Aboard the Wreck of the *Kismet II*, 1955

John Angus Fraser wrote his story fourteen years after the event. He wrote it as something to hold onto during the rough months after his wife Ronie died. The pain of his loss comes through clearly in his story. But what also comes through is a vigorous storyteller at the centre of his tale. We are grateful, as well, to the Rasmussen family of Bay St Lawrence for having encouraged John Angus's writing and for preserving his work.